Harnham
Historical Miscellany

Sarum Studies 4

In tribute to Michael Cowan (1935-2009)

Edited by Jane Howells

Sarum Chronicle
Tanglewood, Laverstock Park, Laverstock,
Salisbury, SP1 1QJ

ISBN 978-0-9571692-2-7

Front cover: West Harnham by Edwin Young (1831–1913), watercolour
(EY158) © Edwin Young Collection

Back cover: Views of Harnham today (Charles Villiers)

Contents

Abbreviations

SJL	*Salisbury & Winchester Journal*
STM	*Salisbury Times*
RCHM(E)	Royal Commission on Historical Monuments of England, *Ancient and historical monuments in the city of Salisbury* vol 1 (the city) 1980, vol 2 (houses of the Close) 1993
VCH *Wilts* 3	Victoria History of the Counties of England, *Wiltshire*, vol 3 1956 edited Pugh & Crittall
VCH *Wilts* 4	Victoria History of the Counties of England, *Wiltshire*, vol 4 1959 edited Crittall
VCH *Wilts* 5	Victoria History of the Counties of England, *Wiltshire*, vol 5 1957 edited Pugh & Crittall
VCH *Wilts* 6	Victoria History of the Counties of England, *Wiltshire*, vol 6 1962 edited Crittall
WANHS	Wiltshire Archaeological & Natural History Society
WANHM	Wiltshire Archaeological & Natural History Magazine
WRS	Wiltshire Record Society
WSA	Wiltshire & Swindon Archives
WSHC	Wiltshire & Swindon History Centre

Introduction

Jane Howells

In 2008 the second in the series 'Sarum Studies' was published, written by Michael Cowan. The label grew from the journal *Sarum Chronicle* to offer succinct, scholarly and accessible local history publications focusing on the suburbs of Salisbury, or on particular aspects of the area in the past. The subject of number two was Harnham Mill, a popular landmark on the western outskirts of the city, now an attractive hotel. While the building may be well-known, its history over some 800 years allowed Michael to indulge his interests in local industrial, architectural and agricultural history to the full. The final chapter in that volume is headed 'Around the Mill' and forms a very brief introduction to the community in the village of Harnham.

Although he was seriously ill, Michael Cowan was already planning another 'Sarum Study' on the villages of East and West Harnham. He had drafted a structure of chapters, written some of the first section, discussed it with friends and colleagues, suggested contributions from others, and done a great deal of 'desk research' on the internet (a late convert to computers, he certainly made the most of the opportunities thereon). Shortly before he died, Michael gave me a capacious carrier bag containing two large files of his notes.

After reading carefully, several times, the contents of the files, and after much thought, and discussion with the other members of the *Sarum Chronicle* editorial team, this collection of essays is offered to readers near and far in tribute to Mike's commitment to the subject of local history and to his home of Harnham. The text that he had written is presented as Chapter 1. We feel that the definitive study of Harnham as a whole deserves an author who can undertake the primary research required, making full use of both Mike's outline and their own ideas and knowledge. We very much look forward to publishing this as a later item in the 'Sarum Studies' series.

Meanwhile we hope the varied contents of this volume will interest and intrigue readers, perhaps enthuse them to undertake research of their own, and certainly tempt them to read *Sarum Chronicle* and the other volumes of 'Sarum Studies'. Those who live in the area might, having read a little about aspects of its history, look at the buildings and streets they see everyday in a new light.

We are delighted that this volume has contributions, most of them published here for the first time, from representatives of the breadth of local history. The subject's true strength lies in its unique characteristic as being equally welcoming to amateur independent researchers, members of local societies, dedicated students, and eminent academics.

Michael Cowan worked for many years for the British Association for Local History. Amongst other innovations he was responsible for initiating their scheme of awards that recognised the special contribution made to the subject by volunteers, both as researchers and writers, and as active participants in their local societies.

It is a particular honour to have two contributions here from

Michael Cowan (right) signing cop of *Harnham Mill,* the mill itself, Ru Newman and Re Sawyer, 2008

authoritative, long-standing people linked to the Association. David Dymond has kindly given permission for us to include the profile that he wrote when Mike retired as General Secretary in 2003. Alan Crosby's skill as editor of *The Local Historian*, his regular pieces in *Local History News,* and his articles in family history magazines (thus bridging a significant divide) will be known to many of our readers. When he heard about this project he expressed disappointment that it wasn't his part of the country, but of course that did not deter him, and we are delighted to have a chapter specially written for this compilation.

The names of four senior and well-known historians of Wiltshire also appear at the head of chapters containing innovative material and ideas.

Medieval Harnham, particularly West Harnham, is described and explained by Tim Tatton-Brown. His expertise as an architectural historian and archaeologist of international repute leads us into the characteristics of this small parish, and demonstrates how the 18th century inclosure map can throw light on Harnham in the Middle Ages. A central focus for the community then and now is St George's church, where modern visitors can still see the 12th century building within later alterations.

John Chandler has taken the entry point to the villages – Harnham or Ayleswade Bridge – and subjected it to the meticulous, thoughtful and often entertaining historical analysis we expect from him. Details of the early river crossings are lost in the mists of time, but John has explored a range of sources to trace the beginnings of the bridge, its chequered history, and its more recent transformation in the 20th century from a dangerous highway to a tranquil place for a stroll. Legal, financial, political, and economic controversies abound.

Adjacent to the bridge is St Nicholas Hospital. Steve Hobbs, archivist at Wiltshire & Swindon History Centre, has used two 15th century cartularies – of the Tropenell family and the hospital itself, to examine the nature and extent of medieval East Harnham. This is not necessarily a simple task because of its close relationship with the parish of Britford. In a typical chalk valley manor, we learn here about some of the residents and their tenements. The sources are rich in topographical detail including field names and uses, and activities such as the extraction of chalk for which the area continued to be known for centuries.

At the beginning of this introduction I mentioned Mike Cowan's Sarum Studies book, *Harnham Mill*. In chapter 6 here, Ken Rogers, former County Archivist for Wiltshire and an acknowledged authority on mills in the region, demonstrates how a different analysis of the evidence indicates that the epithet 'the oldest surviving paper mill in the country' should be applied not to Harnham mill but perhaps to the mill on the other side of the parish, technically in Harnham but known as Bemerton mill.

Had Mike been fit and well, he would no doubt have enjoyed the cut and thrust of debate, and would have graciously acknowledged that information had become available that he had been unable to use. It is a salutary lesson to us all, to get to as many primary sources as possible, to read as widely around our topic as is feasible, but not necessarily believe every word that is written (and published) in any one place. With the passage of time, sources come to light, are listed and catalogued, nowadays often also digitised, and thus contribute fresh knowledge and allow different interpretations than were possible for an earlier generation. Such is the endless excitement of history.

We have also taken the opportunity to include people who have been researching the local area for some years, but might not have seen much of their work in print. Helen Wilcockson has re-written her Open University dissertation on the extension of Salisbury City boundary in 1904 to include East Harnham, introducing a source – the Borough Extension Inquiry – which might well prove of great interest to others for comparative purposes. William Alexander is the Honorary Archivist for the parishes of West and East Harnham. His work on the Miss Warres of Parsonage Farm formed a popular lecture for Salisbury Local History Group and he has here gone the extra mile and turned the talk into a written paper. The short article about Harnham Memorial Hall originally appeared in three parts in the parish magazine, and I have merged them for our purpose here.

In 1996 Michael Cowan edited a volume of letters by John Peniston for the Wiltshire Record Society. Peniston's letters introduce us to a key figure in early Victorian Wiltshire whose Roman Catholic faith did not prevent him from holding public office, despite the formal constraints in place at the time. Though familiar to members of WRS, its volumes might be unappreciated by a wider readership. Some, of course, are very specialised documents; but many of the transcriptions and scholarly introductions bring them within reach of general historians, and should be much more widely known and used. A recent volume is trawled by Ruth Newman for her chapter about William Small in Harnham. His descriptions of life on the Bridge in the 1820s are both very informative and delightful to read. The short final chapter includes some of the references to Harnham in other WRS volumes.

In the 1950s I was a pupil when Miss King was the headteacher at West Harnham Infants' School, and East Harnham Junior School was run by Mr Wood. The infants were housed in wartime Nissen Huts, and juniors were still in the building first erected by Mrs Everett as a gesture of philanthropy to the parish in the middle of the 19th century. It has been a great pleasure to investigate the first hundred years of both these schools. Their logbooks record daily life in all its detail, from the tedium of 'careless mistakes in arithmetic' to the excitement of the fair and races, sadness at the death of a pupil from scarlet fever, and the annual round of weather freezing 'the offices', and 'harvest holidays' allowing the children to work in the fields.

All the authors have provided notes and bibliographies to enable others to follow up their work.

We are grateful to those individuals and organisations who have given permission for the reproduction of illustrations as credited in the captions.

Michael Cowan's whole family has been very supportive of this project and their help has been much appreciated by the editor and other members of the team. My thanks go particularly to Jennifer Cowan for her encouragement.

This fourth volume of 'Sarum Studies' again benefits from the skills and enthusiasm of the *Sarum Chronicle* editorial team, without which the entire enterprise could not continue. I would like to record my gratitude to my colleagues for their work. We look forward to producing further contributions in the series.

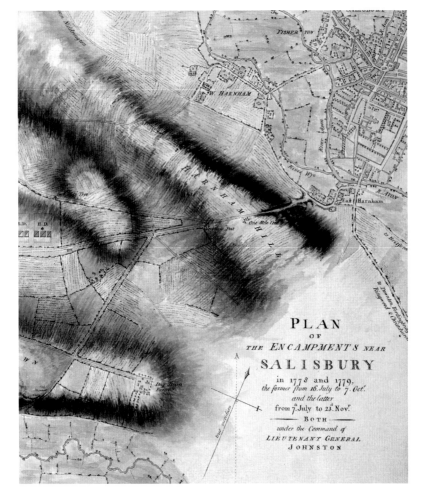

Detail from plan of
encampments near
Salisbury in 1778
and 1779 (see *Sarum*
Chronicle 8 p 33-4

1 Harnham Villages: the beginning of the book

Michael Cowan

Draft outline of chapters prepared by Michael Cowan as at December 2008

10   houses
        1778 ['encampments'] map – growth – 1904 Act –
        Harnham hill – East Harnham – West Harnham
11   churches
        St George's – bells – All Saints – Methodist – Union
        Chapel (now Free Church) – Friends meeting house

The text that follows here was largely written by Michael Cowan, and was certainly not considered finished. He had shown it to Tim Tatton-Brown in April 2009 and incorporated his comments and suggestions. I have made minimal further adjustments, some for clarity or removing typing errors, others in partial answer to queries Mike left such as 'when?' or 'add fn'. It remains in his inimitable style, and stops at the point he reached. He had prepared brief outlines of some subsequent chapters. JH

1 HARNHAM

King George III arrived in Salisbury in 1798 on the way to his seaside holiday at Weymouth and was duly fêted by the civic dignitaries. His party then drove on, completely ignoring the Salisbury Troop of the Wiltshire Yeomanry Cavalry paraded in his honour on Harnham Hill.[1] Where, one wonders, did they find room on the route – up the present Old Blandford Road – actually to parade? Today, what is commonly called Harnham Hill but is more accurately its eastern end, is heavily wooded and quite unlike the natural chalk downland.

This unusual degree of tree cover is the result of building substantial suburban houses on large plots in the later 19th and earlier 20th centuries.[2] Its original state is identified on a 1778/9 map[3] which shows 'one mile tree' at the first milestone on the new Harnham, Blandford and Dorchester Turnpike Trust of 1753-4 part way up the Blandford route and clearly a lone feature in the bare down landscape on which the cavalry could conduct their business. In 1820 John Constable made a pencil sketch of the meadows and cathedral from Harnham Hill with a distinctly bare downland foreground.[4] Vegetation must have been equally sparse, apart perhaps from the odd game covert, when in 1858 Henry Fawcett, later to become an MP and Postmaster General, was blinded in a shooting accident on Harnham Hill.

Modern Harnham is a combination of two originally linear settlements within the ecclesiastical parishes of West Harnham and Britford on the south bank of the River Nadder (often called the Wye or Wylie in earlier maps when it was thought the Nadder only extended to Wilton), and south of the city of New Sarum (or Salisbury). By the 18th century the former royal manor of Britford, corresponding to the parish, belonged to the Earl of Radnor at Longford Castle, downstream on the Avon, while the parish of West Harnham was divided between Radnor and the Earl of Pembroke at Wilton House, upstream on both the Wylye and the Nadder.[5]

Ask anyone living locally now where they live and there will be a strong inclination, perhaps of fairly recent origin, to say Harnham; not East Harnham nor West Harnham. The two had for practical purposes become merged but until 31 March 2009 were effectively disenfranchised, surrounded from east to west by the civil parishes of Britford, Odstock, Coombe Bissett and Netherhampton whereas Harnham was itself simply a Salisbury City Ward, electing two members to Salisbury District Council. It thus had no parish council and no statutory mechanism for considering 'civil parish' issues. There was an informal Harnham Neighbourhood Association with no formal status or powers.

On 1 April 2009 Wiltshire County Council and its four District Councils were replaced by the unitary Wiltshire Council. Salisbury District Council was replaced by Salisbury City Council grouping seven electoral wards each with two or three councillors. The Boundary Commission created one ward as St Martins, Cathedral and Harnham. The southern ward boundary now divides the settlement in a linear fashion rather than reflecting the age-old tithing and ecclesiastical layout. Not everyone was pleased.

The name Harnham derives from the pre-conquest early English as does the separate Ayleswade attached to the ford (wade = ford) and later bridge, built in 1244, when the city of New Sarum was being created. Slightly widened, it is still in use.[6] The well-known tale of how the new bridge diverted traffic from the south and west away from Wilton to New Sarum, to the detriment of the former, needs no retelling here[7] except to the extent that it must have had the effect of enlarging the existing settlement of East Harnham. Six or seven centuries later, and eventually thanks to the 1904 Public Health Act, the present village took on its modern identity as a pleasant suburb of Salisbury.[8]

2 ORIGINS

The first focus to the area was almost certainly the royal manor at Britford – with Harnham, Coombe Bissett and others all, originally in the tenth century, part of the large royal estate. When the first town ('burgh') was built at Wilton, it was important enough to give its name to the new shire county of Wiltshire, a subdivision of Wessex.

Harnham itself can first be identified around 1110 when King Henry I (reigned 1100-1135) the fourth son of William the Conqueror, presented the churches of Coombe [Bissett] and Harnham to Salisbury Cathedral.[9] This was the Norman cathedral at Old Sarum and income from the two churches was used to support a prebend for one of its canons by about 1150 at the latest, a practice consolidated when the cathedral moved to its present site in the early 13th century.

The canon holding the prebend may have built himself a house in the new Close by the mid-13th century but also had the obligation to appoint a priest for the two parishes of Coombe and Harnham and probably built a church in each. The present West Harnham parish church St George's has surviving fabric that suggests it was built in the early 12th century, as does St Michael and All Angels at Coombe Bissett. The priests' most important duty was to take the services but they would also manage the parishes, collecting tithes and accepting legacies or gifts to support their church.

It seems likely that in the later middle ages the title 'parson' was used, the incumbent provided with a house in West Harnham, later to become Parsonage Farm. The present building on the site and nowadays called 'The Old Parsonage' is of at least 16th century origin.[10] The parson then would have appointed a vicar in each parish. In Harnham the vicar occupied a surviving building, 'The Old Cottage' near St George's Church, on the corner of Lower Street and Town Path, clearly marked 'vicarage' on the 1787 map[11] and possibly of 15th century origin.

However there had been earlier occupations than the Anglo-Norman, and evidence of the remains of an iron age agricultural settlement, a Roman road, and a pagan Anglo-Saxon cemetery might suggest continuous human occupation but it is far more likely that each has a finite time span: Iron Age, later second to first century BC, Roman road post AD 43-c 410, Anglo-Saxon,

6th to 7th century. However, modern Ordnance Survey maps show all three features so they need brief explanation.

Iron Age

Iron Age culture marked by the use of iron ploughs and sickles existed in Britain in the later second and first centuries BC. Construction of Harnwood Road in the late 1930s uncovered a site from this period although much of it was destroyed by the road work that had initially revealed it. There was evidence of grain storage pits, and fragments of small ovens used for corn drying or bread making were found in the pit fillings. The excavation report[12] refers to two other similar sites nearby and which, collectively, left little doubt that 'in this district, within a mile of Salisbury, were three, if not more, of these centres of intensive corn production'. These types of sites are now found all over the chalk of Salisbury Plain, possible evidence of a warmer climate. The Harnham finds included large sherds of a pot, a jar, a burnished bowl, and a large storage jar . All the material is in Salisbury Museum.[13]

All this indicates an agricultural economy similar to that extensively explored around Danebury Hill some 15 km to the north east.[14] Here there has been modern excavation of the hill fort and aerial photography of minor settlements at regular intervals to the south under its defensive umbrella.[15] The Harnham site, with those nearby, would fit this pattern. The three nearest sheltering hill forts are Sarum, Figsbury and Clearbury, though none of these has been excavated in the same way as Danebury.

Roman

On the face of it the Roman 400 year occupation of Britain (AD 43-410) passed Harnham by except for their road from Old Sarum or *Sorviodunum* to the south west via Bemerton and Stratford Tony – and nowadays the drive up to the South Wilts Golf Club, a former drove road. The raised *agger* of the Roman road clearly formed the early boundary between West Harnham and Netherhampton. Roman villas, however, had estates, some very extensive. Of those known there are few in Wiltshire and the nearest to Harnham is Rockbourne, 15 km south and described (in its own publicity material) as 'the largest in the area'. It is credible that its estate extended to the Nadder and

Avon settlements. No ford has been identified at Bemerton and any Roman bridge would rapidly have fallen into disuse with the foundations taken for other construction.

Saxon

The evidence for a Saxon settlement in the East Harnham area was found in 1854. Excavations revealed a pagan Anglo-Saxon settlement on the lower scarp slope of Harnham Hill at the top of what was later called, not surprisingly, Saxon Road. Sixty two graves of men, women and children with their grave goods were opened by Mr John Akerman, Secretary of the Society of Antiquaries. An illustrated excavation report was published in the *Wiltshire Archaeological Magazine*.[16] The finds were presented to the British Museum[17] by Viscount Folkstone, heir to the Earl of Radnor. This was before Salisbury's own museum was created. The report lists some 40 of the skeletons and some of their associated grave goods, including weapons, rings, beads, combs, dice, and most unusually a fork.

There was a suggestion that this cemetery relates to the battle fought at Seoroburgh (possibly Old Sarum) in 552AD between the 'indigenous people and the westward encroaching Saxon colonists' and referred to in the Anglo Saxon Chronicle.[18] However the location of the battle, if indeed it did take place at or near to Old Sarum, some four kilometres away, and the nature of the cemetery suggest otherwise, and that it was a straightforward Anglo-Saxon village's burial ground. The presence of grave goods dates it after the 5th century when Anglo-Saxon occupation was starting to spread westwards, and before the widespread establishment of Augustinian Christianity by the mid -7th century when the practice of burying personal possessions with the dead gradually ceased. In short a date in the 6th century is most likely.

There are stone churches of identifiable later Anglo-Saxon origin in the villages of Britford (*c.* 8th – 9th century) and Breamore (10th–11th century) further south along the Avon, suggesting larger and more important settlements, but there is no evidence of a church in Harnham earlier than Norman. The excavation standards of 1854 were poor by what is expected today, and it is unlikely now to be able to establish where there was more of the cemetery to be discovered, although it is quite possible that further graves are there. But the absence of a church building is not necessarily significant; even by the end of the 8th century 'many Christian communities of long standing were still unprovided with any form of church'[19] and priests were permitted to say mass daily 'in the field' where a cross could be raised. Equally an explanation could be that expensive stone was beyond the means of a small community and they settled for timber of which nothing survives.

A discontinuity lies in the fact that the cemetery – and presumably its related settlement – was on the head deposits of the lower downs, possibly about the 40m contour line and well above the riverside alluvium. There are routes on both sides of the chalk valley rivers, (including the five that converge on or just below Salisbury, the Bourne, Avon, Wylye, Nadder and Ebble) along which linear settlements are to be found at intervals, always on terrace, a metre or more above the valley floor and flood plain below. Upstream from Harnham were Netherhampton, Washern (destroyed by the first Earl of Pembroke to improve his view), Burcombe, Barford, and so on; downstream Britford, Bodenham, Charlton and Downton.[20]

3 MEDIEVAL

Turn to a historical encyclopedia[21] and the middle ages are 'a vaguely defined period between say 9th-10th centuries and 15th-16th centuries, according to taste'. Let our taste settle on 1000 to 1500. During this 500 year period perhaps little can be known about a single small place such as Harnham, but it includes a number of national events and developments which has local impact. Forests have been cut down to accommodate the specialist literature – this chapter, in a short local work, will encompass the concept of feudalism, Cranborne Chase, Saint George's Church, New Sarum, and on a less cheerful note, Black Death.

> By the year 1000 central southern England, the heartland of the kingdom of Wessex, was already an ancient settled land, where long centuries of work by prehistoric settlers, the efficiency of Romano-British farmers, Roman land surveyors and road builders and the efforts of Saxon pioneers had laid out the landscape with a framework of estates and villages, towns and parishes, administrative boundaries and ecclesiastical divisions.[22]

Normans brought with them no clear cut scheme of social relationship, Normans entering a well-run English estate would have found little to alter.[23]

Feudalism

Sellars and Yeatman have ingrained '1066 and all that' into the national consciousness. In that year William, Duke of Normandy, arrived to take possession of what, as he saw it, was his and become King William I of England. Most of the lands of the English nobility were soon granted to his supporters. The people of Harnham would have seen at a distance the wooden, and later great stone castle, together with a cathedral, built on the hill fort at Sarisberie, Old Sarum as we now know it.

The occupation was sufficiently secure by 1085 for William to order a national 'stock take', completed within twelve months, to find out how much each landholder held in land and livestock. In Wiltshire there are entries for Cumbe [Bissett], Sarisberie, Wiltune, Bementone, and Bretford, formerly held by King Edward and Edmund son of Aiulf. There are no entries for Harnham or Netherhampton. However, the coverage of Britford, as will become apparent possibly included the tithing of East Harnham, is extensive:[24]

> King Edward held it. It paid tax for one hide [variously estimated as 60 to 120 acres]. Land for 20 ploughs. In lordship 2 ploughs; 6 slaves [villeins]; 10 freedman. 12 villagers, 6 smallholders, and 14 cottagers with 17 ploughs. 2 mills at 20s [shillings]; meadow, 100 acres; pasture 1 league [3 miles] long and ½ league wide.
>
> This manor pays £30 by weight. The woodland is in the King's hands and from it he has 40s in his revenue. Osbern the priest holds the church in this manor, with one hide of land which belongs to the church.

Later there is a further reference to an additional hide.[25]

These entries are notoriously difficult to interpret and locate in modern terms, Osbern's church is still there within the present Britford parish but sites for the two mills are problematic.[26] Nor is it practicable to try and calculate a population – different national attempts finish up millions apart. What such an extract does present is a snapshot of feudal society, the strata, the hierarchy, individuals in total service to the lord on his demesne land (farmed on his own account), others making their own way but still owing service. The Editors of the Wiltshire volume comment 'Domesday Book describes Old English society under new management'. This was feudalism.

The 'framework of estates' of concern here were the tithing, manor and parish of West Harnham and the tithing of East Harnham in the parish of Britford. Tithings were Saxon territorial divisions in the chalk valleys, usually rectangular with the short sides, and boundaries, along the river and the top of the downs, the long boundaries shared with other villages on either side.

Cranborne Chase

Superimposed on this feudal manorial practice was the forest law which severely limited the rights of villagers within its boundaries. Nowadays Cranborne Chase tends to be equated with the more limited modern classification of part of it as an Area of Outstanding Natural Beauty (AONB); historically it was part of the great swathe of royal hunting land that swept from Southampton to Windsor. The New Forest, Cranborne Chase and Clarendon are remnants. Cranborne bordered Holt Forest in the south at Wimborne; the boundary than taking it to Blandford, Shaftesbury, along the length of the River Nadder and then south along the River Avon bordering the New Forest.[27]

Thus the Harnham parishes were contained within the Chase although what practical impact it may have had is impossible to know. Forest laws and officials protected the 'beasts of the chase', including buck, doe, marten, boar, and fox, the last not good news for the downland shepherds protecting lambs; and controlled the rights of agister and pannage (grazing cattle and feeding swine).[28] Royal hunting rights were passed to the Pitt Rivers family in the early 18th century. Local hotels embroider their web sites with references to the hunting exploits of King John.

There was a Harnham aspect of the Chase maintained well into the 19th century at Ayleswade Bridge where 'Deer's antlers are set on a pole, and a chain is across the bridge'. This is said to have occurred from the time of Henry III to 1830 and illustrated by a picture in Salisbury Museum. A toll of cheminage was levied by the owners of Cranborne Chase for 15 days before and after midsummer to discourage travellers who would disturb does during the fawning season.[29]

The Church

St George's Church dominates the village centre of West Harnham.[30] Much straightforward description has been published, mostly deriving from the 1980 work of the Royal Commission on Historical Monuments (England) *City of Salisbury* Vol 1.

New Sarum

The first cathedral and the nearby town of Old Sarum was the main focus until the site of New Sarum in the valley of the River Avon (the Hampshire Avon) at its junction with the River Nadder, opposite Harnham, was determined. The foundation stone of a new cathedral was laid on 28 April 1220; an important occasion not just for the great and good invited from all over the country but for the villagers of the valley settlements, including Harnham. Bishop Poore was probably not as concerned as the modern Environment Agency has been with keeping local people informed on the recent flood defence scheme but no doubt local gossip and the evidence of their own eyes worked just as well. The news was good. For decades the construction work and its associated activities would bring hordes of migrant stone masons, carpenters, carters and other workers.

They all needed accommodation, entertainment and above all food – bread and beer, bringing life and economic growth to the whole area. Corn for bread and barley to be malted for ale had to be included as local crops to make these two staples, to the benefit of the agricultural communities. To what extent this demand could be met is an open question. Was there unused productive land that could be brought into use? Set in a national context at this time however

> … about a third of the tenants in the manorialised area of England lived on the brink of subsistence, along with substantial numbers of the urban poor, particularly since the major industry, production of cloth had been badly hit by Flemish competition.[31]

Salisbury, with its specialist 'ray' cloth weathered the competition until the early sixteenth century but subsistence and poverty were there, and lasted. Life in Harnham and the valley villages was not at all comfortable for those at the bottom of the pile.

Harnham

[H]arnham Bridge with [an]tlers displayed and [m]en collecting chemi-[ca]ge. Oil painting. [?] G Johnson. © [Sa]lisbury & South [W]iltshire Museum

There may have been many corn mills in the area – two listed in Domesday at Britford for example as we have seen. At an early stage in the creation of the city Harnham is recorded as having a fulling [cloth] mill in 1299, well after the establishment of the local cloth industry, but it is likely in earlier centuries to have been a corn mill. A study of the River Bourne identifies eleven mills within some seven miles.[32]

New Sarum's rapid growth may well have outgrown the local milling capacity and prompted the building of the Bishop's Mill still to be seen in the city just above Fisherton Bridge (with the small fast outflow tucked into the corner, not that from the 19th century electricity works, currently a restaurant). The impact on West Harnham was the need to cart more grain, milled or otherwise, into the city, avoiding the long haul around the new cathedral wall by splashing through the two fords at Fisherton Anger.

As a 'planted' city New Sarum has been compared to the modern Milton Keynes[33] although perhaps more dynamic and without concrete cows. Let New Sarum become the more familiar Salisbury and account for its own spectacular commercial success. Within not much more than two centuries, it became one of the top six or seven cities in the country with a population of perhaps some 7–8,000 when 3,000 was considered large.[34] The answer comes down to an enterprise culture and a cloth industry.

Both had an impact on Harnham but the latter was probably more important.

The enterprise culture is illustrated by a specific and documented connection between Harnham and the Pynock family. In the first general entry book of the city of Salisbury, 1387–1452, which recorded meetings of the mayor's court and lists of citizens, there are several Pynock references including one dealing with the 'claims on the land and tenements in West Harnham of the late John Pynock' in 1425. Much earlier, in 1299, Pynocks had owned a 'freehold fulling mill' in West Harnham.[35]

Black Death

However rich and successful Salisbury was in the 14th century it could not escape this pandemic: either bubonic plague, transmitted by rat fleas, or pneumonic by direct infection. Described and measured in many ways, it is invariably considered a demographic catastrophe. It is recorded, with precision, as first arriving in Dorset in August 1348 and reaching London by November followed by three smaller outbreaks; the English population seems generally regarded as having fallen by 50% before 1400.

Salisbury and its surrounding area were in its path and common sense tells us that it could not have avoided the devastating death rate. Indeed although nothing certain is known of its effects locally in 1348, outbreaks in later centuries prompted palliative action, for example preventing strangers entering the city.[36] Coverage in other local histories is sparse and views differ. One early modern commentator offers the thought that Salisbury's popularity with kings and princes 'lies in the fact that this new, comparatively clean and healthy town provided a safe and pleasant resort during the outbreaks of plague that were all too common', after saying that 'it [Salisbury] suffered severely when the Black Death ravaged the whole country ...' and 'The Black Death has created much local unrest'.[37] More recently it has been observed that 'with its damp low-lying situation and water channels Salisbury is unlikely to have escaped the Black Death'.[38]

A national view holds that

> Before the pestilence struck labour was cheap and over-abundant. Landless families sank into destitution but 'within a few seasons, however, the economic situation in the

countryside was transformed. Following the great mortality, estate after estate lacked tenants to work the land'.[39]

The impact of this was that landlords, faced with fractious feudal tenants and expensive hired labour, looked for other ways to farm their estates, and wool was often the solution to supply a developing cloth industry. However in the chalk valleys it was by no means always the answer.

Leaving the medieval period, offers an open question as to whether the local economy suffered from over population, depopulation, or maintained some sort of equilibrium. And it takes us into a series of themed chapters covering aspects of Harnham to the present day.

4 TURBULENCE

The period from the end of the Middle Ages and the start of the Reformation in 1533, until the Restoration in 1660, marks one of the stormiest transitions in English history. In Salisbury it made a lasting imprint. In religion the change from Romanism to Reform, back to Romanism, then to Puritanism and finally to the settled Church of England; in politics from Tudor and Stuart despotism through the all horrors of the Civil War to the Commonwealth and the beginnings of constitutional monarchy … in the surrounding countryside the fall of the monasteries paved the way for the great country houses …[40]

As post medieval centuries passed, peasant and manorial life was little changed unless affected by the impact of major local or wider national events. Locally, West Harnham Mill was built at the beginning of the 16th century, creating a major building site; nationally there was the Reformation of the Church, a century or more later the Civil War, Interregnum and Restoration, and about the same time as that, the innovation of irrigation was a revolutionary change to the traditional agricultural system of all the settlements of the chalk valleys. No one individual would have lived to experience all this but the various impacts of both were long and lasting.

West Harnham Mill

The Mill which still stands as part of the Old Mill Hotel at the southern end of Town Path was built about 1500.[41] In the context of this period the sourcing of material, stone, flint and timber, and the labour force needed to build it, must have had a significant impact on the village.

The squared ashlar (dressed stone blocks) is, in the main, oolitic limestone brought from a quarry at Haslebury near Box in northwest Wiltshire, a distance of 35 miles in a straight line but rather more for ox carts using the probably well-worn track over Salisbury Plain; taking perhaps three days in the process. There was work on the cathedral at this time using the same source of stone. Can one be tempted to think that the odd block fell off the back of a cart? The impact on Harnham came at the final stage of the journey. All this was happening before the drainage of the valley floor was improved by 17th century irrigation so the likelihood is that these heavily leaden carts came across Ayleswade Bridge and through the two villages – all at the two miles an hour pace of the oxen – to the building site on the river.

Timber was needed for the roof. This has not been subjected to scientific testing for age but is as near as it is possible to be certain original. The carpenters took their measurements to the forest and selected trees that could provide the lengths and curves needed.[42] An educated guess suggests [the source to be] Clarendon Forest, still an active royal hunting ground at this time but which must also have been managed for profit.[43]

Because mills are often built across rivers, and hence across parish boundaries, there is sometimes confusion over Harnham's two mills. In the 17th century John Aubrey, traveller and writer refers to a paper mill at Bemerton. This was, and the sluice walls remain, at the Bemerton end of Broken Bridges path but within the parish of West Harnham; active as a paper mill from the 16th to the 19th centuries.[44] It outlived the present mill in terms of production of paper but is of earlier origin and survives.

Reformation

The consequence of Henry VIII (reigned 1509-1547) declaring himself head of the English church in 1529 changed the religion of the country, possibly to the great confusion of those at the bottom of the social pile. Illiterate villagers had to attend church each Sunday on pain of severe punishment. Only someone like a working shepherd might be excused. Prayers were offered in Latin and mass might be said two or three times a year. The congregation benefitted mainly from the visual stimulus of murals showing bible scenes.

Henry followed this by the abolition of the monasteries – including the immensely rich Wilton Abbey which with its wide estates was sold to the first Earl of Pembroke. At this date it appears not to have included the manors of East and West Harnham although later much of Harnham was part of the Pembroke estates until well into the 20th century. Both the manors East and West Harnham were the property of the House of the Scholars of de Vaux (just on the city side of Ayleswade Bridge) and dissolved in 1543 under the Chantries Act. Among other property the manors became the property of Sir Michael Lister.[45]

However there was little impact on services until the Tyndale Bible English translation (1538) and the Prayers and Litany in English (1544) filtered down to parish churches. In 1547 Henry was succeeded by his Protestant son Edward VI who ruled through a Council of Regents during which 'images' were ordered to be removed, together with a ban on vestments, holy water and crucifixes, all causing such a waves of national resentment that preaching was suppressed. Still required to attend, the parishioners were having a totally different experience in a radically altered building. After six years Edward died in 1553 to be succeeded by Mary Tudor (reigned 1553-1558), the strongly Catholic daughter of Katherine of Aragon.

Mary caused any married priests to be dismissed while during her reign some 300 Protestant 'heretics' were burnt. That must have had local resonance as three of these 'Protestant martyrs' (John Maundrel, William Coberley and John Spicer) were executed in this fashion at Fisherton on 23 March 1556[46] – just across the valley meadows from Harnham and an event likely to have been known in the surrounding villages. And presumably some of the Catholic aspects of worship were restored although not for long as Mary died in 1558. Protestantism returned with Elizabeth (reigned 1558-1603), daughter of Anne Boleyn. The Book of Common Prayer was revised, the wearing of surplices and Saints' Days were re-introduced and metrical psalms sung to ballad tunes. Church attendance might have become an altogether more comfortable duty but there is no indication that the wall paintings were uncovered or replaced. One of the treasures today in St George's Church, proudly presented, is a scrap of uncovered 'medieval wall painting'.

Civil War

From 1642 royalist and parliamentary forces fought back and forth across the country. In the south, places like Bristol, Bath, Devizes, Newbury, Oxford, and Wardour Castle near Salisbury all feature on a grand scale.

Compared to these places events did not impinge too strongly on the city itself. It was involved when, at the outset in August 1642, the puritan Mayor and aldermen supporting Parliament took control of arms in the city and started to put its defences in order. Like many towns the citizens' loyalties were divided and the royalists in the Close secretly armed themselves in opposition. Salisbury people suffered from continuous troop movement through the city.

Soldiers needed food and were garrisoned in the town. Skirmishes were frequent; excessive royalist plundering caused outrage while parliamentary troops robbed the cathedral of valuables. However the coming and going of large numbers of men, horses and their baggage damaging property and roads must have been of more significance in the villages.

Possibly the greatest impact on Harnham was in October 1644 when the King entered Salisbury at the head of the victorious army of the South West. Cannon, baggage and a garrison were left at Longford Castle and the main army pushed on in an unsuccessful attempt to attack the parliamentary force at Andover.[47] Of the modern sources only Robertson declares a number: 'In October 1644 Charles entered Salisbury at the head of 11,000 men'. VCH cites Henry Hatcher writing in 1843 but offers no numbers; nor does Wroughton.

Whatever the size of this force, the impact of its arrival on the villages as columns marched over the downs, heading for Ayleswade Bridge must have been alarming. Both armies had well organized systems of either paying for or providing what amounted to a credit note to be cashed in later for food and quartering. However armies move on, and it would be naïve to think that too many actually got paid. Not all the activity of the armies was destructive but baggage trains were essentially for shelters and ammunition not food and fodder. This was early autumn, the harvest was in and grain, bread and animal feed was not lightly to be spared. In Harnham winter 1644/45 might have been leaner than usual.

Later a well-known tale is of a skirmish in January 1645 when a parliamentary force under Colonel Ludlow, holding the Close, challenged a Royalist group entering the city along Castle Street. Ludlow's troops were forced back into the Close and he 'made his escape by Mrs Sadler's house (the King's House) [now the Museum]' – by implication across the river to the Harnham water meadows and over snow capped Harnham Hill. Quite how the people of the village reacted is not recorded.[48]

Irrigation

[this would have linked to a substantial chapter on agriculture] The introduction of floated or irrigated water meadows along all the chalk valleys from the early 17th century meant, paradoxically, better crops and better profits. An immense amount of labour was needed to dig the channels and build the stone control hatches. So once again stone was trundled through the villages. But this time these is evidence that at least some if it came from the Hurdcott quarry some six miles south west of Salisbury.

5 GOVERNING [VILLAGES]

The heading here embraces parishes, manors and villages.

Manors

The functioning of manors, conducted by the Lord's Steward was the form of local government that had also crystalised by 1000 and to which individuals would remain accustomed until modern local government emerged during the 19th century. The Steward presided over the manorial court which controlled many aspects of farming and rural life, attend by leaseholders, tenants of the demesne (where the Lord had given up requiring labour to keeping it in hand), cottages, 'tenants at will' (that is at the will of the Lord) and the more secure copyholders. These were tenants who held their land for a number (normally three) named lives for a very small rent, having paid a large 'fine' or fee on entry or when a name was added.

Manorial custom was based on accustomed use 'beyond the

memory of man'. This determined the conditions of tenure, grazing rights on the common fields, access to wood, stone, and other resources, the level of rents and fines, rights of inheritance and widows' estates. A 'resource' at Harnham, as throughout these valleys would have been the chalk itself, dug for lime to fertilize the arable areas. The varied nature of manorial 'custom' was such that they

> Are not so universal as if a man have experience of the custom and services of any manor he shall thereby have perfect knowledge of all the rest, or he be experte of the customs of any one manor in any one countie that he shall need of no further ensruccions for all the residewe of the mannors within that countie[49]

Manorial custom maintained tight control on common field farming with discipline maintained through fines and the ultimate sanction that an offender could lose the benefit of the common sheep fold on his arable land, that is the common flock would not be available to manure this area on which he depended for a corn crop land, an essential aspect of the sheep corn system. He was nonetheless required to keep his sheep in the common flock, benefitting his neighbours and this losing out on both counts. More demonstrable financial loss is illustrated by the 'presentiment' of a 'homage', not at Harnham but to the Court at Heale, five or so miles upstream on the Avon

> before the Steward, John Poulden, gent, 4 April 5 Jas 1 [1607] ... the homage doe alsoe present John Harford for tyinge of his horses upon the Lynchards[50] in the corne feildes before the corn was rydd contrarye to an anciente order made heere in this Courte and therefore he is amerced iiis iiiid[51]

The real offence seems to be putting the corn crop at risk rather than grazing his horses; and note the plural, more than one horse in an environment where oxen predominated on the land. John Harford was a man of relative wealth but did not escape censure – and a fine of three shillings and four pence which may have hurt more. But many lived as paupers; getting the next meal was an achievement; life was uncertain and sudden death commonplace.

The 'custom of the manor' and its rigid social control created the norms where people could not act as they wished to better themselves other than collectively. Inevitably there were attempts to thwart them. By the mid – 16th century social unrest as beginning to simmer; manorial custom must have been stifling to those with entrepreneurial ambition. The local environment was harsh, potential offences many and varied possible offences subject to severe financial and physical punishment. One individual was summoned for owning more than 20 acres, another claiming to be a wheelwright without having been an apprentice, and a third profiting from buying and selling raw wool instead of making it into yarn for the weavers.[52]

After the Dissolution of the Monasteries William Herbert, 1st Earl of Pembroke and a favourite of Henry VIII, bought the stupendously wealthy Wilton Abbey with its many estates. Whether these included the nearby manors of Harnham and Britford is uncertain but must seem likely. A century or so later, in 1632 there is evidence of a Pembroke manor at Wylye on the Nadder.[53] In 1787 the Inclosure Award for the Parish of West Harnham divides most of it between the manor of the Earl of Pembroke and the Earl of Radnor.

6 AGRICULTURE

The age old traditional agricultural practice of the chalklands was the sheep corn system. Until the introduction of new forms of fertilizer in the 19th century vast flocks of sheep were grazed on the downs and folded in enclosures of hurdles at night on the lower arable land to fertilize the corn crop. The valley meadows offered supplementary grazing early in the year when the downs became bare. The cycle became more complex but dramatically more profitable during the 17th century.

The innovation was promoted by the Earl of Pembroke, at Wilton House, and introduced on all his properties along the Wylye valley. It is not known when the system was built at Harnham but likely to have been by the mid-century. Certainly it was well established in the following century by 1743 when several tenants were presented at the Manor Court for 'not properly working the water meadows' for 'not clearing a ditch' and for 'not repairing the bank of a carrier'.[54] The Manor of West Harnham Inclosure map of 1787 delineates the system at both ends of the parish on either side of the river curve as it touches the southern side but not into the parish of Britford.

7 ROUTES

Speed in his 1611 map of Wiltshire shows a smattering of dwellings around the southern end of Ayleswade Bridge which was to grow into East Harnham and become the hub of several routes into and out of the city. It was located in the long established ecclesiastical parish of Britford. Further west a similar scatter around Harnham church and mill would eventually grow into West Harnham, in the ecclesiastical parish of that name.

A later map of 1778/9 despite its specific military purpose has the unintended consequence of showing possibly the first and certainly the best available early and accurate survey of the roads, farms and cottages of both hamlets.[55] The inclosure map of West Harnham would follow soon afterward in 1787[56] but inclosure at Britford had to wait until 1847 Both show much more detail. To give a very rough idea of scale of the 'encampments' map, the confluence of the River Avon with the 'River Wye' (Wylye) occurs about 200m upstream from the bridge and the two settlements are about one kilometre apart. From the city the road for the south and west [centre right on fig 1] turns right at the south east corner of the Cathedral Close and then left to cross the two arms of the river via St John's Island. On the south bank the road splits.

The main, and strategic, route turns right past what was to become the Rose and Crown Hotel (14th and 16th century origin), uphill around a double bend, then very steeply up what is now known as Old Blandford Road – shaded dark on the map to indicate gradient. The river valley is some 50 m above sea level; 1.3 kilometres south west on top of the downs the 'Direction Post' (bottom left on map) is probably near the modern 110m contour line. A short distance lower down the hill the 'one mile tree' must have been from a different start point in the city.

The Direction Post itself marks a split in the route. Forking right took a traveller along the hilltop drove road, eventually to Shaftesbury and onto the south west; incidentally passing to the south and high above the diminished Wilton. Forking left took the route over the downs into the valley of the River Ebble, eventually via Blandford and Dorchester to Weymouth that King George was in such a hurry to reach.

Back at the bridge a road runs south, past a branch on the left to Britford (now Britford Lane) and then on towards Downton and Ringwood (modern A338). An unmarked fork to the right appears to be on the line of the modern Coombe Road. In the other direction the way out of East Harnham leads north west to West Harnham, for some distance along the bottom of the steep north slope of the Down where the River Nadder curves into the west of its valley. This is the modern Harnham Road (A3094) and it is noticeable that 19th and 20th century development on the left had to cut into the hillside and buildings sit on prominent terraces. On the right houses are level with the roads and mostly their gardens slope down to the high river bank.

Reaching West Harnham this route splits, the left form continuing on to Netherhampton and the right looping through the hamlet with its church of Norman and conceivable Saxon origin. This would develop at the southern end of a valley crossing from the early city suburb of Fisherton Anger, known now as Town Path. At this point the River Nadder has split in two round a large island (now known as the Harnham Water Meadows) involving relatively shallow fords across the two arms and probably an easier crossing than Aegal's ford downstream where the flow from the Nadder and Avon are combined.

The pattern of valley roads and crossings is similar for the length of all the chalk valleys. With minor exceptions there are roads on either side of the river passing through each settlement. Footpaths connect settlements laterally across the valley floor, crossing the river by ford or footbridge – or both. Over time some such lateral crossings have become roads, in some cases major ones. Some remain as footpaths, and a few have disappeared. And with the passage of time the road on one side of the river has developed at the expense of the other. To put it in context on part of the south side of the River Nadder there was Burcombe, Washern until destroyed in *c*1550, Netherhampton, West Harnham, East Harnham and then continuing on the Avon Britford, Bodenham, Charlton and Downton. On the other side Wilton, Quidhampton, Bemerton, Fisherton Anger, Mumworth (Dairyhouse Bridge on the Southampton Road) Petersfinger,

Alderbury, Barford and then Downton – the one settlement that actually crosses the river.

East Harnham

Shortly after the new city was started the ford crossing towards Mumworth was replaced in 1244 by Ayleswade bridge crossing the River Avon just below its confluence with the Nadder – a point later to give its name to Watersmeet Farm and most recently to Watersmeet Road. Two parts of the bridge are separated by St John's Island with originally a travellers' chapel. It attracted traffic away from Wilton and

> the changing of this way was the totale cause of the ruine of Old Sarisbyrii and Wiltoun. For arose this Wiltoun had 12 parish churches and more, and was the hedde town of Wileshir[57]

But East Harnham flourished at the juncture of the bridge and the exceedingly steep Blandford Road (modern road changes have reduced the overall impact of this although it still has an alarming gradient). Much later, in the early 19th century there was an attempt to replace it with something akin to what was later developed as Coombe Road; made less steep by creating a deep cutting.

Extra horses were quite normally added to a team pulling coaches or carts at such locations and it would be very surprising if there was not a thriving business in East Harnham providing such a service. Probably even more difficult and certainly more alarming was coming down. There is no specific evidence but a need for refreshment, particularly drink, might have been uppermost in the minds of carters, coachmen and passengers alike. The modern Rose and Crown Hotel has been there, in some form since the 14th century[58] and doubtless was not the only hostelry.

There are a few illustrations. Possibly the earliest is by Stukeley in 1723 showing Salisbury and Old Sarum from a viewpoint apparently hovering in mid-air over the top of Harnham Hill[59] with a coach and four apparently on the flat but about to go over a lip and plunge to the valley below. In 1827 John Britton's viewpoint[60] is at the one mile post on the Harnham and Blandford Turnpike road (near the modern television mast at the end of

Harnham

Bishop's Drive). His illustration includes a cart with a single horse apparently going uphill and looking surprisingly fresh.

Edwin Young (1831–1913), the well-known local water colourist, painted it as a droveway with sheep moving down followed by the shepherd and his dog. Young's scenes are usually fairly accurate and, unlike some, this one can be located without any doubt. It cannot be dated other than as 'late 19th century', and autumnal colours suggest he knew little about local agricultural practice. Finally, the track surface is better defined in an anonymous view of perhaps about the same time[61] showing a covered wagon drawn by four horses and the carter, probably wisely, on foot.

As Salisbury grew in the 19th century suburbs developed, mainly to the north and influenced by the railway. But by 1900 in addition to the humble dwellings in Harnham's village street there were a few large houses. Harnham House c1830 stood where Newbridge Road now connects with the Downton Road and was demolished in 1970.[62] Harnham Lodge c1800[63] remains hidden at the end of Ayleswade Road, truncated by New Harnham Road. Cliff House at the bottom of Blandford Road, 'a substantial suburban mansion' built in 1835,[64] later used by the Army as Government House, an official residence during the Second World War, and demolished in 1972.

Bibliography

anon, 1854, Anglo Saxon Cemetery at Harnham, *WANHM* Vol 1 pp196-208

Arnold-Baker, C, 1996, *The Companion to British History*, Longcross Press

Bettey, J, 1986, *Wessex from AD1000*, Longman

Bettey, J (ed), 2005, *Wiltshire Farming in the seventeenth century*, WRS vol 57

Carr, David R (ed), 2001, *The first general entry book of the city of Salisbury 1387-1452*, WRS vol 54

Chandler, J, 1983, *Endless Street*, Hobnob Press

Chandler, J, 2008, Two Neglected Early Maps of the Salisbury Countryside, *Sarum Chronicle*, 8, pp33-40

Cowan, M, 2005, *Wiltshire Water Meadows*, Hobnob Press

Cook, H, Cowan, M, and Tatton-Brown, T, 2008, *The Harnham Water Meadows*, Hobnob Press, Sarum Studies 3

Cowan, M, 2008, *Harnham Mill*, Hobnob Press, Sarum Studies 2

Cunliffe, B, 1983, *An anatomy of an iron age hillfort*, Batsford

Dartnell, G E and Goddard, E H, c1894, *Wiltshire Words*, reprinted 1991 by Wiltshire Life Society

Graham, H, 1886, *The Annals of Yeomanry Cavalry of* Wiltshire, D Marples & Co

Greenway, D E, (ed), 1991, *John le Neve Fasti Ecclesiae Anglicanae 1066 -1300 IV*, University of London

Haigh, C (ed), 1985, *The Cambridge Historical Encyclopedia of Great Britain and Ireland*, Cambridge University Press

Harnham Women's Institute, 1954, *History of Harnham*

Hart E, 1957, The Creative Years in Shortt (1957), pp28-53

Hawkins, D, 1980, *Cranborne Chase*, Victor Gollancz

James, T B, 2007, *Clarendon, landscape of kings*, Windgather

Nicolson A, 2008, *Earls of Paradise*, Harper Press

Muir R, 1989, *Portraits of the past, the British landscape through the ages,* Joseph

Musty, J, 1968, Water-mills on the River Bourne, south Wiltshire, *WANHM* vol 63, pp 46-53

Myres, J L N, 1986, *The English Settlements,* Clarendon Press

Newman, R, and Howells, J, 2001 *Salisbury Past*, Phillimore

Piggott, C M, 1939, An Iron Age "A" Site at Harnham Hill, *WANHM* vol 48, pp 513-523

Robertson, D H, 1957, Reformation in Salisbury' in Shortt (1957), pp54-78

RCHM(E), 1980, *Ancient and Historical monuments in the City of Salisbury vol 1,* HMSO

Shortt, H (ed), 1957, *City of Salisbury*, reprinted 1970, S R Publishers Ltd

Stenton, F M, 1985, *Anglo Saxon England,* Clarendon Press

Sumner, H, 1913, *The Ancient Earthworks of Cranborne Chase*, The Chiswick Press

Tatton-Brown, T, 2009, Reconstructing the Medieval Landscape around Salisbury, *Sarum Chronicle,* 9, pp30-36

Thorn, C and F, (eds), 1979, *Domesday Book, Wiltshire,* Phillimore

VCH *Wilts* 6

Wroughton, J, 1999, *An Unhappy Civil War*, Landsdowne Press

Notes

1   Graham, p 22
2   See below chapter 9, Wilcockson
3   Illustration 1 and see also Andrews and Dury 1773, WRS Vol 8 1952
4   Victoria & Albert Museum, reproduced in Cook, Cowan and Tatton-Brown p 37
5   For earlier detail see Cook, Cowan and Tatton-Brown p 14
6   See below chapter 4, Chandler
7   VCH *Wilts* 6, p 3; Chandler (1983) p 126
8   See below chapter 9, Wilcockson
9   Greenway, p 63
10   RCHM(E) building 581
11   RCHM(E) building 584
12   Piggott, pp 513-523
13   SBYWM: 1939.77a, also related 1939.107 and 1937.7
14   The excavations are reported in Cunliffe, 1983, and in the Council for British Archaeology Research Reports nos 52, 73 & 102

15   Cunliffe p120
16   anon, 1854; see also *SJL,* 8 October 1853 p 3
17   registration 1853.1214.1 – 100
18   Myres, p 149
19   Stenton , p 150
20   See also Tatton-Brown (2009) pp 30-36
21   Arnold-Baker, C
22   Bettey, (1986), p 5
23   Stenton, xxix
24   Thorn and Thorn, p 1,6
25   ibid p 67, 58
26   See below chapter6, Rogers
27   Sumner. See also map Tatton-Brown (2009), pp 32-33
28   Arnold-Baker, C
29   Hawkins, p 19. Harnham Women's Institute *History of Harnham* 1954. And see below chapter 4, Chandler
30   See below chapter 3, Tatton-Brown
31   Haigh, p127
32   Musty, pp 46-53. And see below chapter 6, Rogers
33   Newman and Howells, p 21
34   ibid pp 21-22
35   Cowan (2008), p 10 fn 5, 6 Ref Carr, David R (ed), 2001, WRS vol 54
36   Chandler (1983), pp 220-221
37   Hart, pp47-48
38   Newman and Howells, p 21
39   Muir, pp 142, 143
40   Robertson, p 54
41   Cowan (2008)
42   See King C, *Local History News* May 2011 for an example of this skill of carpenters in selecting trees
43   James, many references to timber, but see pp 114-5
44   VCH *Wilts* 6, p 46 n 5; 4, p 245. And see below chapter 6, Rogers
45   Robertson, p 54
46   VCH *Wilts* 6, p 183
47   Robertson, p 71; VCH *Wilts* 6 p 118; Wroughton, p 277
48   Robertson, p 71, Newman and Howells pp 47-8
49   Harleian MS 71 ff45-53 quoted in Bettey (2005), p168
50   Meaning debatable but probably 'a strip of greensward dividing two pieces of arable land in a common field' see Dartnell and Goddard, p94
51   WSA 649/1 (Court Roll of Heale Manor, 1615-32) in Bettey (2005) pp172-5
52   Nicolson, p167
53   Bettey (2005), p236

54   Cook, Cowan, and Tatton-Brown, p 15

55   Chandler (2008)

56   See below chapter 3, Tatton-Brown

57   Leland 1540 quoted in Chandler (1983), p54

58   RCHM(E) building 576

59   Reproduced in Newman and Howells, p1

60   Reproduced in Cowan (2005) p13

61   *Illustrated London News* 31 August 1872

62   RCHM(E) building 578

63   RCHM(E) building 579

64   RCHM(E) building 580

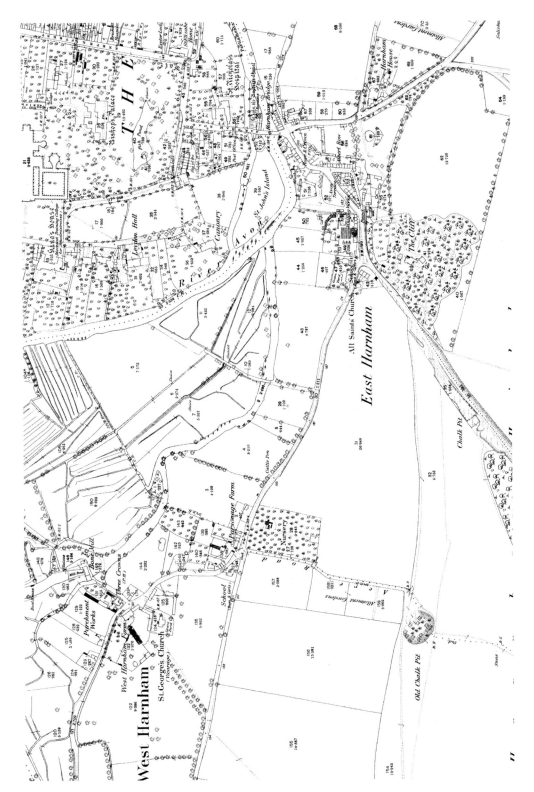

First edition Ordnance Survey 25" map, published 1881

2 Harnham: the name and its meaning

Alan Crosby

'the hoole lordship and maner of olde tyme callid
Haram, otherwise callid East Haram, and now called
Est Harnham, joynyng to Aylyswade brigge over the
ryver of Avene, nowe called Harnham brigge by newe
Salisbury'[1]

In 1936 Oxford University Press published the first edition of
major new work, the highly-influential *Concise Oxford Dictionary
of English Place-Names* compiled by the Swedish place-name
scholar Eilert Ekwall (1877-1964).[2] Scholarly, packed with fine
detail, and supported by half a lifetime's research on linguistics,
etymology and the evolution of names, its 546 pages represented
the first serious attempt to produce a definitive dictionary of the
meaning and derivation of the names of parishes and minor places
in this country. Despite its specialist appeal, the book was a great
success — my copy is a 4th edition, from 1960. But Ekwall was
not always right. Many of the explanations and interpretations
of place-names in his book were swiftly challenged by other
experts, as is usual in the groves of academe. In the ensuing seven
decades new conclusions were reached as a result of more careful
attention to local circumstances, and the bringing to light of
ancient forms of names which provided clearer evidence for how
they originated, a thousand years ago and more.

One such example is Harnham. Ekwall's 1936 explanation
was simple.[3] Perhaps understandably, as he was a Scandinavian
scholar based in Sweden, he looked first at the identical place-

39

name in Northumberland. This belongs to a tiny village 18 miles north-west of Newcastle-upon-Tyne, just off the high road to Scotland. Noting that the name of that village was first recorded as *Harnaham* in 1242, as *Hernham* in 1272, and *Herneham* in 1285, he argued that it was derived from an Old English (or Anglo-Saxon) word *hæren* (or *heren*), an adjective stemming from the word *hær*, meaning 'stone'. Now we encounter a problem: there is no reference to the word *hæren* (or *heren*) in Anglo-Saxon documents. In other words, we have no contemporary evidence for its use or, indeed, its existence. As is by no means uncommon in the work of place-name scholars, Ekwall (a linguistics expert) suggested that there must have been an adjective *hæren*, meaning 'rocky' or 'stony', because it would be logical for such a word to have existed. In fact, he argued this point for a quite different name, Harnage in Shropshire (meaning 'rocky/stony ridge/edge') and then applied the logic to Harnham in Northumberland. There's nothing really wrong with that reasoning. After all, Harnham in Northumberland is in a landscape of pointy rocky knolls and hillocks, and there are crags and basalt outcrops nearby.

But Ekwall, referring to the Wiltshire example of the name, simply states (after giving a couple of early examples of its spelling) that it probably has the same derivation. That, of course, is very much less plausible. Ekwall, like most place-name scholars in the period before the 1960s, did not actually visit the places he wrote about, and had very limited knowledge of landscape, topography or the particular character of individual localities. To him, it was the meaning in linguistic terms, not the logic of the interpretation, which counted. And, also in common with most scholars of his time, he was mainly interested in names which included personal or tribal names, or gave key information about settlement processes and patterns. Landscape names were, to Ekwall and his contemporaries, of much lesser importance. He perhaps imagined that the flat and watery meadows of the Avon *were* a wild and rocky landscape, but more likely was simply not concerned whether or not that was so.

Three years after Ekwall's Dictionary was published, the 16th volume in the English Place-Name Society's county series appeared. *The Place-Names of Wiltshire* was edited by J E B Gover, Allen Mawer and F M Stenton. This indefatigable trio had been working assiduously since the mid-1920s, when Mawer, professor of English at Liverpool University, founded the Society. They had worked on, among other counties, Hampshire, Hertfordshire, Middlesex and Sussex. Stenton was soon to emerge as the most celebrated Anglo-Saxon historian of the 20th century, and all three were conversant with the landscape, Anglo-Saxon culture, and pre-Conquest history of Southern England. In the Wiltshire volume they firmly and authoritatively dismissed Ekwall's explanation, stating that his 'suggestion of a lost OE adj. ＊ *hæren*, is ruled out by the topography'.[4] Although they conceded that the actual derivation was 'uncertain', they proposed instead that the name is from the Anglo-Saxon, or Old English, *hara*, meaning 'a hare'. There was, they suggested, the possibility that the genitive plural form of the noun, *harena*, was involved. This would translate literally as 'of the hares' or, more loosely, 'where hares were found'.

Given the meaning of the second half of the word, this interpretation seems very plausible. The place-name element *hamm* has a variety of implications and senses. The greatest place-name scholar of our own time, Margaret Gelling (1924-2009), analyses the term in rich and fascinating detail, identifying how other writers have come up with at least six major meanings:

1. 'land in a river bend'
2. 'a promontory of dry land into marsh or water'
3. 'a river meadow'
4. 'dry ground in a marsh'
5. 'an enclosed plot, a close, cultivated land in a marginal place'
6. 'a piece of valley-bottom land hemmed in by higher ground'

Based on her unrivalled knowledge and understanding of how our Anglo-Saxon and early medieval forebears viewed the physical world which they inhabited, Margaret Gelling herself felt strongly that the first four of these were far more likely than the last two. However, always a pragmatist, she realised that this simple term could easily have changed its meaning over time, or varied in its implications between different parts of the country. Nevertheless, she identified clear 'common characteristics' which helped to isolate the basic meanings of the word.[5]

To us, of course, it is immediately clear that the place called Harnham in Wiltshire has — or 15 centuries ago must surely have had — characteristics of all four of the favoured meanings. It stood beside the bends and meanders of the Avon and Nadder; it was where dry land on the south bank came close to the water (hence the location of the vital 'Aylyswade brigge over the ryver of Avene, nowe called Harnham brigge by newe Salisbury'); there was drier ground in what were in Anglo-Saxon times wetlands and marshes; and it had riverside meadows, those same meadows that Mike Cowan loved so much and wrote about so eloquently.

Combining the two elements, therefore, produces the place-name *harena-hamm*, 'the watery meadows where hares were found' or 'the riverside lands frequented by hares', a beautiful image of how the landscape appeared to our Anglo-Saxon forebears who coined the term a millennium and a half ago.

In some of the medieval documents which refer to the Harnhams the genitive plural form of the noun, *harena*, is apparent from the spelling and, by implication, the pronunciation. Thus in 1358 Richard de Walton, the parson of Rochford in Essex, and others, were involved in a judgment concerning title to land against John de Nevill, an Essex knight. It centred on a great scattered portfolio of landholdings in ten English counties, including Wiltshire.[6] The case produced a standard medieval form of documentation, a 'foot of fine' ('fine' is from the Latin, *finis*, because it was the final judgment in the case, 'foot' because a copy of the decision was written out at the bottom of the document and then detached for filing in the rolls of the Court of Common Pleas in London). Among the places in Wiltshire mentioned in the 'foot of fine' were *Westharenham* and *Estharenham*. In medieval English pronunciation there were no silent letters, so each syllable of these two names would have been pronounced in full (thus, *Est-har-en-ham*). There is an obvious similarity to the Anglo-Saxon genitive form, pronounced *har-ena-ham*).

Other sources confirm that in the early medieval period this was one of the conventional forms of the name. A foot of fine from a hearing of 1289 at Wilton, concerning the lands held by William le Dun, deceased, granted a life interest to his widow, Benedicta, and on her death they were to go to their son John. The property comprised three messuages, three virgates of land, and an annual rent income of 8 shillings, all in *Westharenham*. As a token rent for her occupation of the estate, Benedicta was to pay her son a rose on the feast day of St John the Baptist (24 June).[7]

At the same time, however, other spellings and thus pronunciations are apparent. In 1249 the king's justices came to Wiltshire to conduct an *eyre*, a court sessions hearing cases from across the county, the forerunner of what was shortly after this date to become the assizes. Among the numerous cases which they heard, the justices learned that recently Adam the Swineherd, who was suffering from 'falling sickness', had suddenly dropped dead outside the door of Netherhampton church. They had to determine whether a crime had been committed (so were acting in effect as coroners, giving a verdict on the cause of death). Their decision was 'misadventure', but the townships of Netherhampton and *Harham* were fined because they should have sent representatives to be present at the hearing, but had failed to do so.[8]

At the same sessions of the eyre, another case — even more tragic — was heard. Robert, the chaplain of *Harreham* was reported to have hanged himself in his house at *Harreham*. The body was discovered by the chaplain's son Thomas (an interesting indication that priestly celibacy was not yet strictly enforced). It was also recorded that a stranger had been found dead in Langford, and the judges determined that this was murder by persons unknown. The townships of *Langeford*, Britford, *Harreham* and *Odestok* did not send representatives, and were fined for that offence.[9] From these brief accounts of ancient tragedies we learn, quite incidentally, much about local place-names.

Clearly in the middle of the 13th century many people in the area were pronouncing the name either as *har-ham* or *hara-ham*, and the clerks to the court wrote down the approximate phonetic version of what they heard. Another example occurs in the documents from almost a century later, when in 1326 Edith, daughter of Philip Buterstip, and Edith her sister (there's a cause for domestic confusion!) were involved in a land dispute with Simon de Wyly, concerning two parts of one messuage and a virgate of land in *Estharham*.[10] This form of the name certainly survived into the late-16th century. Thus, in 1582 John Yonge of Durnford and his son and heir, Edward, became heavily indebted, and as part of the ensuing legal process an extent (or inventory) was made of their landholdings. This listed, among other properties, six tenements in *Eastharam*, implying that the shortened form of the name was still current.[11] The quotation which begins this paper was written shortly after this date. It states that the name was 'of olde tyme callid Haram, otherwise callid East Haram', but was now called East Harnham, which seems to confirm that the earlier forms died out in the years around 1600.

Throughout the period from the 14th century onwards, the modern spelling and pronunciation were evident, but they gradually gathered status until in the 17th century emerging as standard. Seven centuries ago this process was perhaps helped by the fact that an important, and literate, man used that spelling for his surname. John de Harnham is mentioned in numerous Wiltshire documents (and many from beyond the boundaries of the county) in the reign of Edward III, and the spelling of his surname, and that of his immediate descendants, is well-nigh consistent. Thus, in 1332 Edward III issued a national tax demand, the 'fifteenth and tenth', and for Wiltshire two officials, Hildebrand de Londone and John de Harnham, were appointed to oversee the collection of the king's revenues. In the taxation list which they drew up the community of Harnham is given its modern spelling, and 36 householders are listed by name, contributing a total of 60s 6¾d.[12]

John de Harnham and Alesia his wife, leading county figures and important local landowners, are often named in documents, and from the 1330s onwards the name as they spelled it becomes increasingly frequent. It appears in that form regardless of the language of the document itself, for there was no feasible way of converting English place-names to Latin or French forms. For

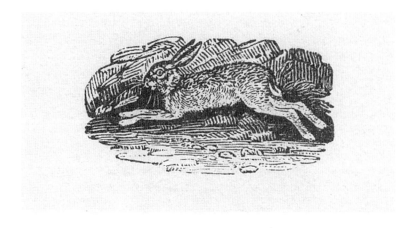

example, on 17 May 1330 William Lynford, the lord of the manor of East Harnham, granted to one of his tenants '*de pastura xxiiij° porcorum in stibulis camporum de Est Harnham*' ('the pasture of 24 pigs on the stubble of the fields of East Harnham).[13] Six decades later, Henry Calne granted land in East Harnham to his daughter Alice Coleman and her husband Henry, including *duas dimidias acras terre arab[ilis] jacentes in campo de Est Harnham, quarum una dimidia acra jacet in furlongo qui vocatur Lynchlond juxta terram Oliveri Harnham* ('2½ acres of arable land in the field of East Harnham, of which half an acre lies in the furlong called *Lynchlond* next to the land of Oliver Harnham').[14]

Anglo-French was still used for title deeds and land grants until the end of the fourteenth century. In 1377, for example, a Wiltshire cartulary, or collection of charters, made reference to *lez villes de Estharnham et Westharnham, in le Counte de Wiltes,*[15] while in March 1388 Thomas Lynford, lord of East Harnham, granted John France *une mees de vynt ut pees de longe et desuys de bien edefee sur le commune de Estharnham, terme de sa vie* ('a piece of land 28 feet long on which he may build, on the common of East Harnham, for the term of his life').[16]

Thus, of the three possible forms and pronunciations of the name which were current in the 14th century — Harham, Harenham and Harnham — the latter emerged as the eventual winner. With the middle 'e' silent the name became easier to say, but by retaining the 'n' it preserves the presumed genitive plural of the Anglo-Saxon word, 1500 years later. But that's about the technicalities of etymology. To my mind, the lovely abiding image is of a pastoral idyll: the hares, leaping and gambolling on those riverside meadows, observed with interest and perhaps amusement by those Anglo-Saxon colonisers seven centuries before the soaring spire of the cathedral rose into the sky.

Bibliography

Conyers, Angela (ed), 1972, *Wiltshire extents for debts Edward I–Elizabeth I.* WRS, vol 28

Crowley, D A (ed), 1989, *The Wiltshire Tax-list of 1332,* WRS, vol 45

Davies, J S, (ed), 1908, *The Tropenell Cartulary: being the contents of an old Wiltshire muniment chest,* vol 2, WANHS

Ekwall, Eilert, 1960, *The Concise Oxford Dictionary of English Place-Names* 4th ed, Oxford University Press

Elrington, C R, (ed), 1973, *Abstract of feet of fines relating to Wiltshire for the reign of Edward III.* WRS, vol 29

Gover, J E B, Mawer, Allen, and Stenton, F M, 1939, *The Place-Names of Wiltshire,* English Place-Name Society, vol 16

Gelling, Margaret, 1984, *Place-Names in the Landscape,* Dent

Meekings, C A F, 1961, *Crown pleas of the Wiltshire Eyre, 1249.* WRS, vol 16

Pugh, R B, (ed), 1939, *Abstracts of feet of fines relating to Wiltshire for the reigns of Edward I and Edward II.* WRS, vol 1

Notes

1   Davies, 212
2   A brief biography and list of published works is given at http://en.wikipedia.org/wiki/Eilert_Ekwall.
3   Ekwall, 220
4   Gover, 222
5   Gelling, 41–50
6   Elrington, 114–115
7   Pugh (1939), 32
8   Meekings, 247
9   *ibid*, 250
10   Elrington, 17
11   Conyers, 39
12   Crowley, 17
13   Davies, 176
14   *ibid*, 233
15   *ibid*, 188
16   *ibid*, 190

3 Medieval Harnham

Tim Tatton-Brown

Harnham is first mentioned in the 'Register of Saint Osmond' when King Henry I granted the churches of Coombe (Bissett) and Harnham to Salisbury Cathedral (then at Old Sarum) sometime between 1107 and 1135. Soon afterwards, the income from these two churches and from some land in Boscombe was used to create a new prebend in the cathedral, and the arrangement was confirmed by Henry II in 1158.[1] The name Harnham is clearly an Anglo-Saxon one though its meaning is uncertain,[2] and there was definitely a settlement in the area on the gravel terrace south of the river Nadder by the 7th century. This was shown by the discovery and excavation in 1854 of an Anglo-Saxon cemetery of over 60 graves just below Harnham Hill, which contained a variety of pagan objects.[3]

From the 11th century, the whole area south of the Nadder and west of the Avon was within the outer bounds of Cranborne Chase, a vast area of about 800,000 acres, which was controlled by the king and the lordship was granted out to various close followers. So William II (Rufus) granted it to Robert Fitzhamon, whose daughter Mabel inherited it. She married Robert, Earl of Gloucester, an illegitimate son of Henry I and, from this time at least, the Chase was often treated as a forest.[4] As a result it came under the infamous Forest Law, which would have caused problems to those living in Harnham and many of the other settlements around the north, south and east sides of the city of New Sarum in the 13th century.[5] It is ironic that when this city was being laid out for the bishop between the 1190s and the early 13th century the owner of the Chase was John, Earl of

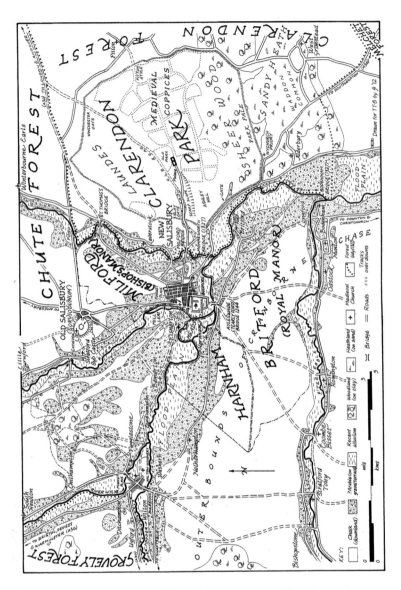

Harnham in the me eval landscape arou Salisbury, drawn by Atherton ©

Gloucester, who became King John in 1199. The barons' revolt and Magna Carta were therefore intimately connected with the area.

In the extreme north-east corner of the outer bounds of Cranborne Chase was the large Anglo-Saxon royal manor of Britford and, as the boundaries of the parish clearly indicate, the later parish of West Harnham must have been cut out of the north-west corner of Britford, possibly at the time when Henry I was granting the church to Salisbury Cathedral. The early

12th century was the time when the manorial boundaries were being used to define the boundaries of the English ecclesiastical parishes; these boundaries then remained, mostly unchanged, until the 19th century. It is significant that the parish of (West) Harnham did not extend all the way to the major fording place of the river, Ayleswade,[6] and that this area immediately south of the new city always remained part of Britford parish, even after Bishop Bingham paid for the great stone bridge there in 1244-5.[7] Only later is it called Harnham bridge, and only really in the 18th century was the suburb of 'East' Harnham created, with its own church in 1854. A place called 'East Harnham' probably did not come into existence until the post-Medieval period.[8]

Turning now to the parish of West Harnham itself, we can see that it is a 'classic' Salisbury Plain parish with chalk downland to the south, a large gravel terrace in the centre where the arable was, (situated on the fourth terrace of the Avon at about 150 feet above sea-level), and an area of alluvium on the flood plain to the north. A large meander in the river Nadder creates an area of alluvium to the north of the river (now Churchfields) which belonged to Fisherton Anger on the east and Bemerton on the west. The alluvium to the west and east of this, south of the river, were the two distinct areas of water meadows that belonged to West Harnham, with the meadows to the north-east uniquely mostly lying in a separate island between the two equal branches of the Nadder. This allowed two watermills (Fisherton and Harnham mills) to operate in tandem throughout the later Middle Ages,[9] and a track must have run between them. By the 18th century the track was a raised causeway, now the Town Path.

Across the centre of the gravel terrace runs a major road, and it is clear that in the Middle Ages most of the dwellings or crofts in West Harnham were situated along this road, even though they were all abandoned later (see below). The road runs east to Britford (and later to Ayleswade Bridge, and New Salisbury), and west to Netherhampton, Bulbridge and on to Shaftesbury.[10] A loop road came off the main road to the north, to run to the church, mill and river (Lower, Middle and Upper Streets), and it is interesting to note that where this returns to the main road it is opposite the principal and wide drove road that led due south to the downland. Called Carrion Pond Drove (there was a pond in the middle of the lowest part of the drove but sadly this area has now been encroached upon by the Brethrens' Meeting Hall and new houses) this track still survives today though very overgrown and barely used. From the late Middle Ages the drove also served as access to a large chalkpit though this ceased in the mid-20th century. It is perhaps worth noting that in the cathedral fabric accounts for September 1480, there are references to money paid to Thomas Whyte and other labourers 'for breaking the chalk at Harnham quarry for the work of new vaults' (the crossing vault in the cathedral). A stone-mason, Richard Cooke, is then paid 'for stopling le chalke at harnham quarry,' and a few days later Robert Nycolas of Harnham is paid for the carriage of 10 cart-loads of chalk from Harnham quarry to the Cathedral cemetery.[11] Carrion Pond Drove was clearly also in use in the later Middle Ages as the principal route for sheep being taken to the large area of open downland on Harnham Hill. Sunken lanes (now paths) at the base of the hill at the southern end of Carrion Pond Drove show where the sheep were driven up and down There is another smaller way to the downs further west, called Foxmore Drove.

Along the southern boundary of the parish, and just behind the highest point of Harnham Hill (at 353 feet above sea-level) is the Shaftesbury Drove. This was a major through route by the early post-medieval period, running along the top of the downs and west to Whitesheet Hill, which was briefly a Turnpike road (from 1761-87).[12] Its earliest depiction as a road is in Ogilby's atlas of 1675,[13] and it too is likely to have been used as an important route in the later medieval period. It should, however, be noted that although the whole of the western boundary of the parish of West Harnham is marked by the 'agger' of the Roman road leading from Old Sarum to Badbury Rings, never in the Middle Ages was this 'agger' used as a road,[14] as there cannot have been a crossing point of the Nadder (or the Avon) to Old Sarum after the Roman period. No place-name reflects this, though further south-west the 'stratford' (an Anglo-Saxon place-name) at Stratford Tony is mentioned, indicating a post-Roman ford. In the Roman period it is likely to have been a bridge.

The one other key document for understanding the topography of Medieval West Harnham is the 1787 inclosure map.[15] This shows that the principal manor, owned by the Earl of Pembroke, was centred on West Harnham Farm, just to the north of the parish church. Lord Pembroke owned much of the land in the eastern and western parts of the parish, but in the centre a new 'sub-manor' of West Harnham Walronds had been cut out of it, based around Walrond's Manor Farm. In 1787 this manor was owned by the Earl of Radnor, and the earlier history of the manors is not known. On the east side of the parish, and running south from the Nadder along the parish boundary, is land belonging to Parsonage Farm. More land belonging to the Parsonage can be found in the centre of the parish, as well as on the open downland and the meadow areas in the north-west corner of the parish. This land is probably the property that was attached to the prebend of Coombe and Harnham; the Parsonage Farm estate was not finally broken up and sold until 1910.[16]

One of the most interesting details on the 1787 map is the whole series of croft names (18 in all) along the main east-west road through the centre of the parish and mainly on the south side. These almost certainly relate to dwellings with attached arable fields, which were abandoned in the later Middle Ages. By 1787 the population in the parish had diminished very considerably, with only a small number of houses with small gardens in Upper, Middle and Lower Streets remaining. After the Black Death and in the 15th century many areas of regular 'tofts and crofts' (ie houses with an attached piece of arable land) on the gravel terraces of the south Wiltshire valleys were abandoned. These sites are often still marked by earthwork remains.[17]

In Harnham it is very unfortunate that almost all the 'croft' sites marked on the 1787 map have been built on again in the 20th century without first having an archaeological excavation. It would be nice to know when the crofts were first built and then when they were abandoned, and only excavation will answer this. However, it is likely that this abandonment occurred in the later Middle Ages, with the occupants moving to the bridgehead settlement at East Harnham or into Salisbury itself, by then the sixth or seventh largest urban centre in England.[18] The crofts were, perhaps, first made here in the 12th or 13th centuries.

Apart from the crofts along the main road, and the small dwellings in Upper, Middle and Lower Streets, there were probably three other major house complexes in the parish. These were West Harnham Farm, just to the north of the church, Walrond's

Buckler St George's
church West Harnham
from the south-west.
1803
©Wiltshire Heritage
Museum, Devizes

Manor Farm, and Parsonage Farm. The oldest was probably
West Harnham Farm where the original manor house dating
from at least the early 12th century must have been situated.
Unfortunately no ancient house now survives here. At Walrond's
Manor and Parsonage, by contrast, two fine historic buildings
do survive, and one day a detailed analysis of both should throw
light on these important centres within the parish. The thatched
vicarage on the corner between Middle and Lower Streets may
date from the 17th century.

The most significant building in the parish was, of course,

Buckler St George's
church West Harnham
from the north-east
1803
©Wiltshire Heritage
Museum, Devizes

the parish church, and this fine little structure survives to the present day, albeit heavily restored in 1873-4 by the well-known Victorian architect William Butterfield.[19] He completely rebuilt the east and west walls of the church and added a new porch on the south side. Before this, in about 1830, the north tower had been almost entirely reconstructed. Luckily there are watercolours by John Buckler of the church from south-west and north-east in 1803,[20] and these show us something of the church before the drastic alterations.

Despite all this, we still have the shell of the nave and chancel from the early 12th century, and it is likely that when the church was given to Salisbury Cathedral by Henry I it was newly built.

Detail of 12th century doorway (photograph Laura Shapland)

On the north side of both the nave and chancel there are round-headed original windows with chalk-block dressings.[21] Evidence survives that the earlier (smaller) chancel arch had a stone altar on its south side, as there is still part of a 13th century wall-painting in the recess above. Even more remarkably, the 12th century north doorway to the nave also survives, with its chalk voussoirs and inset tympanum. There is also a pair of carved capitals and hollowed-chamfered abaci above the original nook-shafts. Unfortunately this doorway is now rarely seen because, despite continuing in use as the main entrance into the church (beneath a later medieval tower-porch) until the 19th century, it is now hidden within the vestry. Original chalk-block quoins can also still be seen externally at the junction between the nave and chancel on both the north and south sides.

That the parish only had a small population in the Middle Ages is confirmed by the fact that the nave, the people's part, was never enlarged. As we have seen, a tower-porch was added on the north in the early 14th century (rebuilt in the 15th century from the evidence of the 1803 watercolour), and at about the same time the chancel arch was enlarged and rebuilt. Probably a little later in the 14th century a south chapel, well-made and faced with ashlar, was added to the nave, possibly at the expense of one of the holders of the manor. It has fine windows on the east and south with trefoil-headed lancets, a beautiful ogee-headed piscina,[22] and a rare squint window in the west wall, which was perhaps made to allow people outside the church to observe mass being celebrated.[23]

In contrast to the fine churches in Salisbury, no rebuilding of this church took place in the late Medieval period, once again suggesting that few people lived in the parish. The chancel was, however, given a new wagon roof in the later 15th century, and this has moulded wall-plates, and ribs with carved bosses and busts beneath. The cost of this work must have been paid for by the canon at the cathedral who held the prebend of Coombe and Harnham. One of the most prominent of these canons in the late 15th century who might have provided the finance was Lionel Woodville, the brother of King Edward IV's Queen Elizabeth. He was given the canonry by Bishop Beauchamp (1450-81) and held it from 1467 to 1478,[24] before going on to become bishop himself in 1482.

By the end of the Middle Ages, therefore, we must think of the parish and manor of West Harnham (containing an area of 1,179 acres[25]) as having a very small population, but with rich downlands, covered in money-producing sheep, to the south, and good areas of arable in the centre, much of it presumably under the control of the manor, particularly after the demise of the 'crofts and tofts'. To the north the fine water-meadows or 'wet-meads' were already being drained (initially perhaps by the millers) and used for hay crops. [26] In the summer the meads were divided into strips for haymaking, traces of which can still be seen today. At this time, also, the very beginnings of a new system of 'floating' the meadows in early Spring was starting: a subject that Michael Cowan was to make his own.[27]

Bibliography

Clark, P, and Slack, P, 1976, *English Towns in Transition 1500-1700,* Oxford University Press

Cook, H, Cowan, M, Tatton-Brown, T, 2008, *The Harnham Water Meadows,* Hobnob Press

Cowan, M, 2005, *Wiltshire Water Meadows,* Hobnob Press

Greenway, D E (ed), 1991, John Le Neve, *Fasti Ecclesiae Anglicanae* 1066-1300 IV, University of London

Horn, J M, (ed), 1962, John le Neve, *Fasti Ecclesiae Anglicanae 1300-1541,* III, Salisbury Diocese, University of London

Ogilby, John, 1675, *Britannia,* Osprey reprint 1971

RCHM(E), 1980, *Ancient and Historical monuments in the City of Salisbury vol 1,* HMSO

Steele, N and Tatton-Brown, T, nd, *The Harnham Water Meadows, a brief history.* Friends of Harnham Water Meadows Trust

Tatton-Brown, T, 2009, 'Reconstructing the medieval landscape around Salisbury' in *Sarum Chronicle* 9, 30-36

VCH *Wilts* 4

In WSA at WSHC

A1/210/115/EA27 Inclosure map, Harnham 1787

776/90, Parsonage Farm, cottages and land in W Harnham, land in Britford, Sale Particulars including map for auction on Tuesday 31 May 1910

Notes

1   See discussion in Greenway, D E (ed), 1991,   John Le Neve, *Fasti Ecclesiae Anglicanae* 1066-1300 IV, University of London, 63

2   See above chapter 2 Crosby

3   Recorded in the very first volume of the *Wiltshire Archaeological & Natural History Magazine* 1854, 196-208

4   Poole, E H L, 1959, 'Cranborne Chase' in VCH *Wilts* 4, 458-460

5   See chapter 4 for the imposition of 'cheminage' at Harnham Bridge; also Hawkins, D, 1980, *Cranborne Chase,* Gollancz, 19, 35

6   The ford at Ayleswade probably replaced the Anglo-Saxon ford at Britford, after first the great Royal park and palace of Clarendon were created, and then the city and cathedral close of New Sarum.

7   See below chapter 4, Chandler

8   See below chapter 9, Wilcockson

9   See below chapter 6, Rogers

10   In the post-medieval period this road was blocked by the Earl of Pembroke's park at Wilton

11   Tatton-Brown, T, 1998, 'The building stone for Salisbury Cathedral', in *Hatcher Review,* Vol V no 45, 42

12   Cossons, A, 1959, 'Roads' in VCH *Wilts* 4, 254-271

13 Ogilby, John, 1675, *Britannia*, Osprey reprint 1971, pl 26. It is worth noting that horse-racing was already taking place on the downs in the south-west corner of the parish in 1675, as Ogilby shows 'the (grand) stand'. See also VCH Wiltshire 4, 370-82 for further details of horse-racing here from the 16th century. John Chandler also points out that the Shaftesbury Drove road may be that shown stylistically on the c1370 Gough Map

14 The use of the Roman road would have ceased in the early 5th century when the urban centres and settlements were abandoned. See my essay Tatton-Brown, T, 2009, 'Reconstructing the medieval landscape around Salisbury' in *Sarum Chronicle* 9, 30-36

15 WSA A1/210/115/EA27 Inclosure map, Harnham 1787. See p174

16 WSA 776/90. Sale documents and map for auction on Tuesday 31 May 1910. See also chapter 8, Alexander, on the Miss Warres, residents of Parsonage Farm

17 For example in the neighbouring Ebble valley around Bishopstone. See oblique air photograph in Hare, J, 1994, 'Agricultural Rural Settlement in the chalklands of Wiltshire and Hampshire from c 1200 – c 1500' in Aston, M, and Lewis, C, (eds), 1994, *The Medieval Landscape of Wessex*, Oxbow Books, fig 7.2, 162

18 Clark, P, and Slack, P, 1976, *English Towns in Transition 1500 – 1700*, 83

19 RCHM (E), 1980, *City of Salisbury*, HMSO, 43-44

20 Buckler albums, WANHS library, Devizes ii, fo 35

21 They were probably rediscovered and unblocked in 1873

22 There is also a fine 13th century trefoil-headed piscina in the chancel

23 The church was dedicated to St George, while the south chapel's altar was apparently for the Holy Trinity. RCHM (E), 1980, 44, note 2

24 Horn, J M, (ed), 1962, John le Neve, *Fasti 1300 – 1541*, III, Salisbury Diocese, University of London, 46. See also Ross, C, 2000, *The Canons of Salisbury*, Dean & Chapter of Salisbury Cathedral, 150-1

25 1178.679 acres according to the OS Map, to be precise

26 Steele, N and Tatton-Brown, T, nd, *The Harnham Water Meadows, a brief history*. Friends of Harnham Water Meadows Trust

27 Cowan, M, 2005, *Wiltshire Water Meadows*, Hobnob Press; Cook, H, Cowan, M, Tatton-Brown, T, 2008, *The Harnham Water Meadows*, Hobnob Press

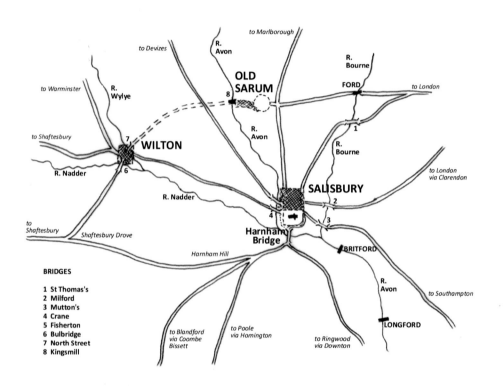

Sketch map showing Harnham bridge in relation to Salisbury and Wilton roads and rivers
© John Chandler

4 Harnham Bridge

John Chandler

Incredible as it may now seem, until 8 March 1933 all traffic heading south from Salisbury towards Ringwood or Blandford passed over the medieval Harnham Bridge, and until the later 18th century most journeys between London and the south-western counties went this way too. Harnham Bridge, whether or not its builder envisaged it so, was to play a crucial role in the medieval and later city's success as a commercial hub, and gave it the competitive edge over its older rival, Wilton. This paper draws on an unpublished history of the bridge's neighbour, St Nicholas's Hospital, written c1713,[1] and on local and national archives, to explore some facets of its history which, if not entirely forgotten, seem to have been overlooked by recent accounts of Salisbury.

Harnham Bridge was built before 1244 by the second bishop to regard New, rather than Old, Sarum as his episcopal seat, Robert Bingham (bishop 1228-46).[2] On this southward development of Salisbury Close, Bingham built St Nicholas's Hospital, a chapel of St John, and the bridge. That much is clear, and is repeated in every history of the city. What was there before is far from certain. An alternative name, Ayleswade Bridge, had been in common use by 1413 and explicitly identified with the present structure by 1471,[3] and that name is recorded in documents from the mid-13th century. It means 'Ægel's ford', and is probably much older than the first document to record it, because both elements of the name are Anglo-Saxon in origin. *Ægel* as a personal name occurs in several important places, including Aylesford in Kent, and the county town of Buckinghamshire, Aylesbury. 'Wade', from the Saxon word *gewæd*, is an archaic alternative for the more common Saxon word, ford, both words (as in modern English) implying a crossing through, rather than over, the river.[4]

So there was a fording-place before – perhaps several centuries before – the bridge and city were built, and, by implication, roads leading to it from either side. But it is unclear where the ford was, and whether or not it had been replaced by a bridge before 1244. Neither of the two apparently ancient north–south road alignments responsible for Salisbury's plan, High Street and Catherine Street, are aiming for Harnham Bridge; one is heading 100m upstream, the other 150m downstream. There was a tradition in the 18th century that Cow Lane, probably the present Friary Lane, led to the earlier crossing, which would place it some 300m below Harnham Bridge;[5] and Henry Hatcher in 1843 seems to have believed that Ayleswade Bridge and Harnham Bridge were different structures which co-existed at least into the 14th century.[6]

He was probably mistaken. It is true that the outer bounds of Cranborne Chase, allegedly drawn up shortly before 1200, some 50 years earlier than the present construction, referred to *Aylwardesbrigg*; but the document as it has come down to us is a later version, which could have been amended.[7] Writing *c*1713, Edmund Hickman tells us that before Harnham Bridge was built, 'there was at first but one wooden bridge for foot passengers [pedestrians]; all on horseback (as all waggons, carts, coaches, etc.) went through the water'.[8] This arrangement was not uncommon on minor rivers,[9] and in Wiltshire had given Trowbridge ('the wooden bridge') its name before 1086.[10] A narrow medieval stone bridge across the River Ebble next to a ford survives near Salisbury at Coombe Bissett, and more challenging river-crossings down the Avon from Salisbury may be inferred from the names Britford, Longford[11] and Fordingbridge.[12]

Hickman and Hatcher provide no convincing evidence for their assertions, and even if based on more than guesses, the local topography suggests that the only place where one could 'wade' the river was at , or very close to, the site of Bingham's 1240s construction.[13] In common parlance the name Ayleswade Bridge had become attached to this medieval Harnham Bridge by 1413,[14] so it is likely that a bequest of Thomas Boyton to the maintenance of Ayleswade Bridge in 1400 refers to the present structure, not a precursor.[15] By this period, too, we find references to *le Brigghelonde* and *Briggeforlong* in terriers of the common fields of East Harnham, and these appear to lie adjacent to the king's highway leading to Odstock.[16]

Established as it was in the bend of a major river, the Avon, close to the confluence with two others, the Nadder and Bourne, Salisbury relied on its medieval bridges – St Thomas's, Milford, Harnham, Crane and Fisherton – for access from every side except the north. To the Harnham crossing, in particular, roads converged from various directions, Ringwood via Downton, Poole via Homington or Odstock, Blandford via Coombe Bissett, and Shaftesbury via Harnham Hill. Moreover, Bishop Bingham's Harnham Bridge was correctly seen, especially by the disgruntled burghers of Wilton, as having changed the regional road pattern, by diverting traffic between London and the south-west through Salisbury, to the detriment of Wilton's and Old Sarum's passing trade. The earlier route from the east is conjectured to have used the Roman road approaching Old Sarum, crossed the Avon at Kingsmill Bridge, Stratford sub Castle, and the Wylye and Nadder respectively by North Street bridges and Bulbridge at Wilton.[17]

The oft-quoted remark of John Leland, made some three centuries after the bridge was built, that 'the chaunging of this way was the totale cause of the ruine of Old-Saresbyri and Wiltoun',[18] can only be partly true, as Wilton was in quite steep decline before 1200;[19] it is, however, testimony to the longevity of the impoverished town's grudge. But Bingham's masterstroke was by no means unprecedented. The bridge over the Trent built at Newark in the 1130s, also by a bishop, damaged Nottingham and Lincoln; that over the Thames at Abingdon damaged Wallingford; medieval Lichfield's success was attributed to its causeway and bridge.[20]

We speak of Harnham Bridge – in fact it is two bridges joined by a raised causeway. The longer, southern, bridge crosses the mainstream of the Avon with six pointed arches of 14ft span on average, is 119ft long, and was probably about 15ft 6in wide when built.[21] The shorter, northern, bridge is now of two arches, 10ft 9in and 16ft 7in span, and is 77ft long; a third arch, on the northern approach from the city, has been filled in, and there may have been a fourth.[22] This bridge spans what appears to be an artificial channel, creating an island on which St John's chapel and other buildings sit. The task of building an arched structure was not in itself a major challenge to the medieval mason – a much grander arched structure was in progress, after all, as the centrepiece of the neighbouring Close. The problem lay in establishing firm foundations and a stable structure in flowing water. Consideration of how this was achieved gave rise to an ingenious theory current in the 18th century. It may have originated with Francis Price, cathedral clerk of works, who in his 1753 book noted:

> Whoever will take the trouble of carefully inspecting the two bridges at Harnham, may find reason to conclude, that the northern one was built upon dry land, and that a cut was made from it upwards, high enough to take the waters of Avon, Nadder, and Wyly, and convey them through the said bridge to some distance below; which being done, they were enabled to make a bay across the original river southwards, and to build that southern bridge also on dry land; then the bay was demolished, and the rivers resumed their original channels.[23]

The projector of a medieval bridge had to ensure, not only that it was competently and sufficiently built, but also that provision was in place for its maintenance and survival. Bingham in 1245 appropriated the church at Burstock, West Dorset, the revenue from which was to maintain the bridge; he also acquired a house and half-acre of land at Harnham close to the bridge to maintain it and St John's chapel.[24] The lands with which St Nicholas's hospital were endowed were to be used, not only for the proper uses of the hospital, but also in repairing and mending the bridge.[25] And in 1244 he placed responsibility for the bridge, chapel of St John and hospital of St Nicholas upon the dean and chapter, who in turn appointed Walter of Wylye the first warden of the bridge.[26] The bishop's intention was presumably, in line with chapels beside or on bridges elsewhere,[27] that the chaplains of St John's, supported by the hospital, would say masses for travellers and receive offerings to pay for bridge repairs. Indeed, the historian of St Nicholas's, Christopher Wordsworth, asserted that this was what happened right through the middle ages:

> For three hundred years exactly – from 1244 to 1545 – the salaries of the priests that officiated there, and the repairs of the bridge itself, were paid by the masters of St Nicholas,

who recouped themselves with the offerings made by pious wayfarers who turned aside from the road to this wayside chapel.[28]

But this was by no means the case. In 1259/60 the dean and chapter returned responsibility for the hospital (but not the bridge or chapel) to Bingham's successor as bishop, Giles of Bridport, thereby divorcing oversight for the hospital and bridge.[29] Thus in 1312 the hospital's master could claim that he was not responsible for repairing the bridge, which was then fallen into ruin and broken.[30] Piecemeal repair may have relied on bequests by Salisbury citizens, aware of its vital role in maintaining the city's economy. Thomas Boyton's legacy in 1400 was preceded by others as far back as 1318.[31] The bridge may not, in fact, have been in too bad a state in the 14th century since, unlike its neighbours Milford and Kingsmill, complaints about it never occur in Ancient Indictments or Coram Rege rolls between 1327 and 1400.[32]

This was to change in 1413, when three leading Salisbury citizens were granted pontage for seven years, the right to collect tolls from users of the bridge, in order to repair its ruined, broken and dangerous state.[33] The grant's preamble observed (as was customary in such documents) that, 'no-one in law is responsible for repairs to the bridge, so it is said', and charged the dean (presumably because most of it lay within the liberty of the Close) with oversight of the citizens' work. The tolls to be levied were graded, giving a useful insight into the kinds of traffic using the bridge:

> for any kind of waggon carrying goods or merchandise for sale, one halfpenny;
> for every quarter of grain and rye for sale, one farthing;
> for every two quarters of beans, peas, malt, oats and salt for sale, one farthing;
> for each horse, mare, ox, cow and calf for sale, one halfpenny;
> for every ten sheep, goats or pigs for sale, one penny;
> for any consignment of bread, garlic, onion and fish for sale, one halfpenny;
> for any tun (252 gallons) of wine for sale, one penny;
> for any pipe (126 gallons) of wine for sale, one halfpenny;
> and for all other merchandise and goods for sale not here specified, conveyed across the foresaid bridge (apart from

wool, leather and sheepskin), one penny per £1, one halfpenny per 10s, one farthing per 5s.

Two points should be noted: the ordinary wayfarer, walking or riding, appears to have crossed the bridge toll-free; and the pontage grant was of limited duration – seven years while the bridge was put into repair. No further pontage grants to Harnham Bridge are recorded in the medieval patent rolls, so we are to assume that the tolls lapsed c1420. But they recur, inexplicably, a century or more later. Following the dissolution of the monasteries during the 1530s William Herbert, who became earl of Pembroke in 1551, built up an estate based on the lands of Wilton Abbey, but including also property confiscated by the crown from Margaret, countess of Salisbury, who was executed in 1541.[34] This included the borough of Wilton, lands in the town, and, 'all the tolls, customs and profits of whatever kind arising from the bridge called Harnham Bridge which were accruing to her ...'[35] This right to tolls seems to have become attached to the borough of Wilton, and was no fiction. A 1562 Pembroke estate account book includes against the heading Wilton borough, tolls of Harnham Bridge 20s.[36] And in the c1565 survey of Pembroke estates, among the earl's revenue from Wilton properties that had formerly belonged to the countess of Salisbury, there is an entry against the mayor and burgesses of Wilton for 20s for the toll, customs and other profits from the bridge called Harnham Bridge currently put out to lease.[37] There was in fact a much earlier precedent for a toll of this kind levied by one community on the bridge of another; the burgesses of Cambridge in 1275 took tolls on Whittlesford Bridge, six miles to the south.[38]

Hickman, writing c1713, knew of this toll. He recorded that Wilton borough had granted a lease for the right to collect the toll to one Ralfe Tunstall in 1629/30, and that in his own day a lease was in force to one Fisher, and that, 'a barr have been shot through upon refusal of toll.'[39] Hickman did not know why Wilton had this right to a toll, which he thought applied mainly to salt carts, but he surmised that at certain times of the year a toll may have been paid to St Nicholas's, which the earl of Pembroke had appropriated for the use of his borough of Wilton. The toll on salt continued as a folk memory as late as 1825, when James Harris referred to it as being in force into the 17th century for repairing the bridge.[40]

In the Wilton borough records there is in fact a document of 1682 which may help to clarify the mystery.[41] It asserts that by ancient right the mayor and burgesses were entitled to certain tolls on traffic over Harnham Bridge, and authorising three named individuals (presumably the lessees) to collect them. The tolls were restricted to cart loads of salt heading towards Salisbury (for which they levied a gallon of the salt, but paid the carter 'a canne of beere' [*sic*] and a halfpenny loaf, or one penny in lieu); also a fourpenny toll for every cart load of fish heading for Salisbury and one penny for every horse load of fish.

What seems curious about this toll is that there is no suggestion that the proceeds should be used to repair the bridge, and, as we shall see in the recurring maintenance disputes of the 17th century, Wilton was never held responsible for repairs. But this toll has a number of similarities with another levied at the bridge, cheminage through Cranborne Chase. Cheminage was a forest owner's right to levy a toll on travellers passing through his forest and, since the rivers Avon and Nadder formed the southern boundary of the chase, anyone crossing Harnham Bridge or Bulbridge at Wilton was *de facto* entering or leaving the forest jurisdiction.[42] Cheminage was taken at these bridges, and complained about by local inhabitants, from the 13th century onwards,[43] although by the 17th century it seems to have been discontinued at Bulbridge, and levied at Harnham Bridge only during what was known as the 'fence' month, mid-June to mid-July. This was the fawning season for the does, and was presumably continued in order to diminish the traffic passing through the chase which might disturb them.[44] To signify that cheminage was being levied buckhorns were displayed on the bridge, and the

n and elevation of
rnham Bridge, late
h century (WSA
/533/2/3, f 109)

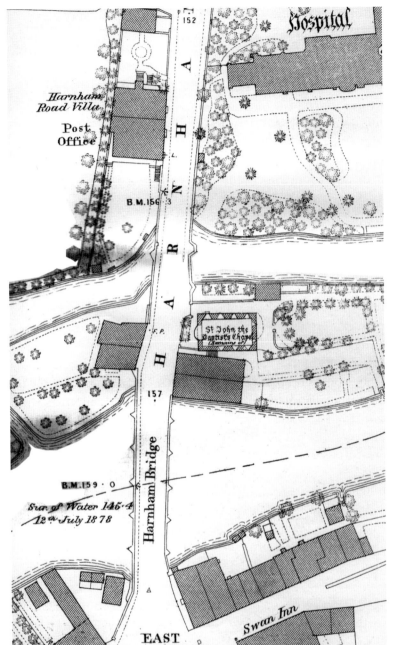

Ordnance Survey large-scale plan of Harnham Bridge are 1879 (sheet Wilts. LXVI.15.14, publish 1880, at 1/500 origi nal scale)

steward of the chase granted a warrant to a collector to levy 4d for any waggon, cart or carriage, and 2d for any horse.[45] A newspaper description of the custom, published in 1848, two decades after Cranborne Chase was disfranchised, claimed that the cheminage had been 4d for a cart and 1d for a horse, precisely that claimed as toll by Wilton borough.[46] This similarity, coupled with Hickman's remark that the Wilton toll may only have been taken at certain times of year, and the fact that cheminage was also taken at Wilton's principal bridge, Bulbridge, suggests a link — but how Wilton borough could claim a toll on Harnham Bridge remains a mystery.

In 1530 Henry VIII's Statute of Bridges placed responsibility on local magistrates (including powers to collect rates from local inhabitants) for the maintenance of bridges whose repair was not otherwise provided for.[47] Although Harnham Bridge does not feature in the earliest surviving Wiltshire quarter sessions records from the later 16th century,[48] between 1622 and 1692 its ruinous condition was repeatedly presented to the magistrates in sessions.[49] Underlying these complaints was a long-standing dispute over who was liable for its repair. In fact the wrangle over Harnham Bridge could be used to illustrate how a law intended to safeguard bridges had the opposite effect, in that the bridge was neglected by all parties, so anxious were they not to set a precedent that they should be responsible for maintaining it.

In about 1600, Edmund Hickman informs us (taking the hospital's side in the argument), Mr Bee, a Salisbury alderman, laid 'divers loads of stones and gravel' on the bridge, and Bishop Cotton (bishop 1598–1615) had also undertaken repairs; in 1608 eight loads of flint were laid on the bridge, presumably by the hospital since the cost, £1 6s, appeared in the accounts. Then in 1610 Mr Bigge, master of the hospital, while repairing his stable:

> pulling down an old [wall] did cause or suffer to be carried for the several loads of stones and rubbish laying it on the bridge and about the highway near it that being the nearest and most convenient place for him to dispose of it, about which time also Dr Barneston and Dr Hide prebends of the church of New Sarum [ie the cathedral] did cause to be laid (at their own proper cost and charges) several new stones upon the said bridge where the greatest decay was, and the said Mr Bigge did what he did for conveniency only, and not as any duty of his place as master of the hospital.[50]

Although happy to own up to flytipping, therefore, Bigge pleaded not guilty to repairing the bridge. But when he left the hospital the incoming master, Dr Matthew Nicholas, was indicted at the 1636 Salisbury assizes, along with the dean and chapter and the neighbouring country to repair the bridge, under penalty of £50.[51] Nicholas was minded to sue Bigge for dilapidations, according to Hickman, and had he done so that would have admitted the hospital's liability. But instead he contested the order against the hospital, and was successful, for the time being at least.[52] In desperation Wiltshire quarter sessions in 1641, because the bridge, 'is now growen in greate decay for want of raparacion

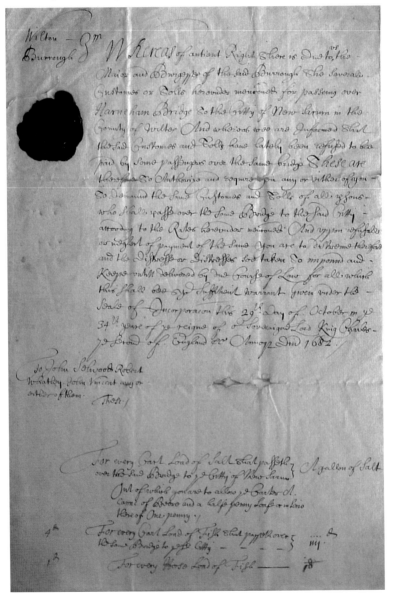

Wilton borough record of 1682 authorising toll collection on Harnham Bridge (WSA G25/1/179)

for the the upper part of the same bridge is worne even to the ribbs thereof,' paid for the speedy mending and repair of the upper part, on condition that the expense would be repaid once it was established who was responsible for the bridge and no precedent was set.[53]

The magistrates were not prepared to let matters rest. In 1640 they summoned Nicholas to Salisbury guildhall to answer charges that 'certain lands were given for the repairing of Harnham Bridge which as is informed remains in your occupation and hath not been imployed by you accordingly.'[54] They were aware that certain lands in Dorset (ie Burstock) as well as Wiltshire were involved, and that this fact had been concealed. They tried to make enquiries, but were thwarted by bureaucracy because two counties (and therefore jurisdictions) were involved. In 1653 and again in 1660 they paid for further emergency repairs, all the while pursuing the hospital, and denying that their actions set any precedent.[55]

The hospital meanwhile maintained its defence, based on various arguments as shaky as the bridge had become. Other parties besides the hospital had repaired the bridge in the past. The master had discretion as to how money from the hospital's endowments was spent. When the hospital was refounded in 1610 there was no mention in the charter of repairing the bridge, and the hospital had in any case lost part of its income. The bridge had been so strongly built in the first place that it had never needed repair until 30 or 40 years previously, There were in any case two bridges, and it was unclear that the founder had intended them to repair the greater, as their land only extended as far as St John's island. The chapel of St John was a chantry chapel and, by analogy with other such chapels on bridges, the chaplains were responsible for repair. Since the chantry chapel was dissolved by the crown (in 1548), the crown or any purchaser from the crown (ie William Herbert), should pay for repairs.[56]

The persistence of successive masters in pursuing these arguments seems to have been successful. The county paid for further repairs in 1670,[57] and in 1685 a rate was set for the repair of Harnham Bridge, to which the borough of Chippenham (which can have derived no benefit from it) contributed 10d.[58] Writing c1713 Hickman noted that the bridge had been repaired at the county charge within these ten to twelve years.[59]

Thus it was that Harnham had become a 'county bridge', the responsibility of the magistrates meeting in quarter sessions, and of the county surveyor whom they appointed. This responsibility extended beyond the bridge itself to the roads extending 300ft (100yds) on either side.[60] In Harnham's case this seems to have included the Downton, Blandford and Salisbury roads, since an 1859 schedule noted 388yds of road (the bridge itself would account for about 88yds).[61] Consequently when turnpike trusts were enacted to oversee and improve Salisbury's main road network in the mid-18th century, they all stopped short of the bridge.

The first, in 1753, was sometimes confusingly referred to as the Harnham Bridge Road,[62] because its title began: 'An act for repairing and widening the road leading from Lobcomb corner in the parish of Winterslow, to Harnham Bridge in the county of Wilts ...'; in fact its main concern was the Salisbury to Southampton road. This was followed in 1756 by the Harnham Hill to Blandford Trust, and in 1766 the Whitesheet Hill to Harnham Trust, which turnpiked most of the old downland route between Salisbury and Shaftesbury. The Downton road was never a turnpike. The Blandford and Shaftesbury turnpikes met at the top of Harnham Hill, and traffic for Salisbury used the Old Blandford Road to descend to the bridge; the present Coombe Road was not constructed until after 1846.[63] The downland Shaftesbury route's turnpike act was not renewed when it expired in 1787, and thereafter the present A30 valley road via Wilton became the preferred route west from Salisbury.

The improvement of the roads which the bridge served led to renewed complaints about the bridge itself.[64] In 1772 it was presented as being in decay and in need of repair, 'and that it would be convenient and proper to widen the same'. The magistrates accordingly advertised in 1773 for tenders to undertake the work, but perhaps no satisfactory contractors emerged. For in January 1774 the contract was awarded to Lord Folkestone (the prinicpal

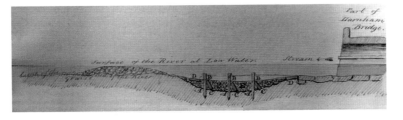

Sketch by Daniel Alexander, 1809, showing the effect the bridge's inadec apron on the river downstream (WSA A1/110/1810E)

landowner), Sir Alexander Powell (newly appointed recorder of the Close) and Henry Penruddock Wyndham (a leading Salisbury magistrate). These three unlikely building contractors were, therefore, acting much like the trustees of a turnpike trust, whose activists very frequently were the local landowners with the most to gain financially from any improvement. For £450 they contracted to repair the bridge and the adjoining roads, to widen the carriageway on the bridge to at least 20ft, with 1ft thick parapets, 4ft high, and to provide a 10-year guarantee. An inscribed stone survives on the northern bridge commemorating this work.

Running below the main (southern) bridge on the west side is a pavement, known as an apron, made to prevent the river in spate from undermining the arches. Price mentioned it in 1753, and believed (perhaps implausibly) that it was later than the bridge, and intended to divert water through the northern channel so as to deepen it for navigation.[65] Following floods in c1803 and 1809 a surveyor's report concluded that the apron did not extend far enough downstream and a large hole had developed in the riverbed which needed to be professionally filled if the bridge were not to be in danger of being washed away.[66] One of the contractors who undertook this work, and which cost the county £770, was a certain John Peniston.

Peniston (c1778-1848) became a prominent Salisbury architect, but more importantly for the bridge, he was appointed county surveyor for Wiltshire in 1822, and was succeeded in that role by a son, John Michael (died 1858) and a grandson, Henry, who between them held that office until 1864.[67] The family home was in De Vaux Place, a stone's throw from the bridge, and on the schedule of county bridges drawn up by Henry in 1859 Harnham Bridge heads the list.[68] Its condition during this period must have been under constant surveillance, and we hear of no mishaps to the bridge itself, although it was the scene of occasional suicides and tragedies.[69] There was a popular interest in the antiquity and significance of the bridge at this time,[70] and in 1851 it added to its achievements a minor distinction in English literature. The fledgling novelist Anthony Trollope, while still employed by the Post Office, recalled in his autobiography how he: 'stood for an hour on the little bridge in Salisbury, and had made out to my own satisfaction the spot on which Hiram's

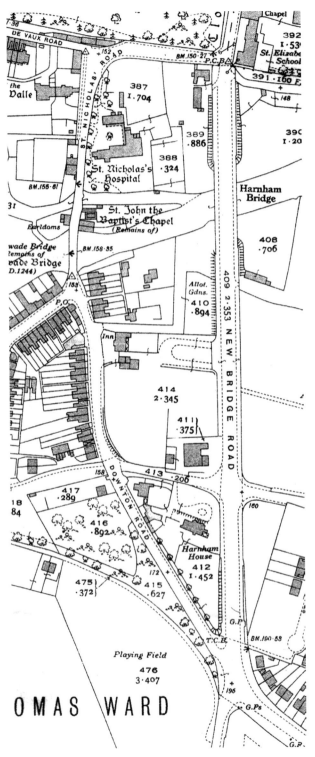

Ordnance Survey plan, 1937, showin[g]
old and new bridges (sheet Wilts.
LXVI.15, 1937 revision, at 1/2500
original scale)

hospital should stand'.[71] This he claimed was the inspiration for *The Warden*, the first of his Barsetshire novels. From the later 19th century a very fine plan and elevation of the southern bridge has survived.[72]

In 1888 the responsibility for major bridges passed from Quarter Sessions to the newly formed Wiltshire County Council, and in 1904 Salisbury's municipal boundary was extended to include East Harnham, thus bringing the whole bridge within the city.[73] This could have had disastrous consequences for Harnham Bridge. In 1906 the city council implemented a sewerage scheme for Harnham, which included laying a 9-inch cast-iron pipe within the roadway of the bridge.[74] Believing (wrongly) the bridge to be its property and responsibility, the city council employed contractors to begin trenching work, which they did with pickaxes, wedges and sledgehammers. Work was halted after the trench had passed the second arch from the south, when the county council became aware of it and claimed the bridge as its own. The county called in an engineer to report on the possible damage, and he concluded that the joints of the arches and stones may have been shaken and the bridge seriously weakened. The work was allowed to proceed, provided the remainder of the trench was carefully chiselled out, and the city signed a legal agreement with the county to indemnify it against any future expense which could be attributed to the hamfisted sewer excavation.

The final chapter in Harnham Bridge's career, prior to its honourable retirement, began in 1922. In April Salisbury city tried to persuade Wiltshire county to pay equal shares for straightening out the right-angled bend by the Close wall north of the bridge, claiming that the traffic at this point is very heavy and almost continuous.[75] They failed, but in December 1923 the Salisbury town clerk wrote again to the county, pointing out the great danger to pedestrians using Harnham Bridge because of the congestion caused by vehicular traffic. The footpaths are very narrow and if two vehicles pass each other on the bridge there is not sufficient room left for pedestrians. Either a new bridge should be built or a scheme to widen the existing bridge implemented. The county prevaricated during 1924, although a site meeting was held in April and another arranged in November. A new bridge was the preferred option, opinion having been swayed partly by an objection by the Society for the Protection of Ancient Buildings to widening the existing bridge. Negotiations and planning dragged on through the 1920s, and it was not until September 1930 that work commenced.

The new bridge and road, 1,650ft long with a 40ft wide carriageway, was designed by Sir Owen Williams and built by Fothergill Brothers of Exeter.[76] It takes a straight line from Exeter Street to the junction of the Blandford and Downton roads, and is some 400ft shorter than the route by the old bridge. It was completed in January 1933 at a cost of about £33,000 (largely paid for by the Ministry of Transport), and officially opened at a ribbon-cutting ceremony on the bridge on 8 March 1933. During construction all other Salisburys in the world were invited to contribute a stone for the new bridge, but this bright idea seems to have foundered and a commemorative plaque was incorporated in the eastern parapet instead. One feature of the new road, which had to be explained to those attending the ceremony was a 'round-a-bout' at the Blandford and Downton road junction, intended to slow down traffic. This usage of the word is first recorded (in Glasgow) in 1929, so would have been unfamiliar to most Wiltshire residents.[77]

Soon after the new bridge opened Salisbury Chamber of Commerce proposed that it be called Broadway and Broadway Bridge. Salisbury City Council debated the matter and came up with New Bridge and New Bridge Road. The town clerk wrote to Wiltshire County Council, who bluntly replied that the name Harnham Bridge was already in place on the plaque on the new bridge. And so from July 1933 the new bridge was officially to be known as Harnham Bridge (although New Bridge Road has been retained), and the old one (according to the town clerk) Aylesward Bridge – a perversion of Ayleswade not recorded by the editors of the English Place-Name Society.[78] This old bridge of Harnham, now with its venerable name of Ayleswade Bridge restored, remains in leisurely use, by vehicles controlled by lethargic traffic signals, by Harnham pedestrians, and by a select minority of tourists who saunter south of the cathedral Close.[79]

Bibliography

Andrews, J and Dury, A, 1773, *map of Wiltshire*. A reduced facsimile appears in WRS vol 8, 1952, edited by E Crittall

Benson, R, and Hatcher, H, 1843, *Old and New Sarum, or Salisbury*, J B Nichols

Chandler, J, 1987, *Salisbury and its Neighbours*, Salisbury Civic Society

Chandler, J, 2004, Where was Old Sarum?, *Sarum Chronicle 4, 22-30*

Chandler, J, 2007, Deconstructing Wilton, *Sarum Chronicle 7, 56-63*

Coates, R, 1989, *The Place-Names of Hampshire*, Batsford

Cockburn, J S, 1976, *Western Circuit Assize Orders 1629-48*, Camden Society, 4th series, vol 17

Cowan, M (ed), 1996, *The Letters of John Peniston ... 1823-1830*, WRS vol 50

Cunnington, B H, 1932, *Records of the County of Wilts*, George Simpson & Co

Davies, J S (ed), 1908, *The Tropenell Cartulary: being the contents of an old Wiltshire muniment chest*, vol 2, WANHS

Dryden, A, 1906, *Memorials of old Wiltshire*, Bemrose & Sons

Duke, E, 1837, *Prolusiones Historicae, or the Halle of John Hall*

Flower, C T (ed), 1923, *Public Works in Medieval Law, vol 2*, Selden Society vol 40

Gelling, M, and Cole, A, 2000, *The Landscape of Place-Names*, Shaun Tyas

Goldney, F H, 1889, *Records of Chippenham*, Diprose, Bateman & Co

Gover, J E B; Mawer, Allen, and Stenton, F M, 1939, *The Place-Names of Wiltshire*, English Place-Name Society vol 16

Harris, J, 1825, *Copies of the Epitaphs ... in Salisbury Cathedral*, Brodie & Dowding

Harrison, D, 2004, *The Bridges of Medieval England*, Clarendon Press

Howells, J and Newman, R (eds), 2011, *William Small's Cherished Memories and Associations*, WRS vol 64

Jervoise, E, 1930, *Ancient bridges of the south of England*, The Architectural Press

Johnson, H C (ed), 1949, *Wiltshire County Records: Minutes of Proceedings in Sessions 1563 and 1574 to 1592*, WRS vol 4

Jones, W H R & Macray, W D (eds), 1891, Sarum Charters and Documents, Eyre & Spottiswoode for HMSO, Rolls Series 97

Ledwich, E, 1771, *Antiquitates Sarisburienses*, printed and sold by E Easton

Price, F, 1753, *Observations on the Cathedral Church of Salisbury*

RCHM (E), 1980, *Ancient and Historical monuments in the City of Salisbury vol 1*, HMSO

Riley, B, 1995, *Highways and Bridges: abstracts from the 17th century Wiltshire Quarter Sessions Great Rolls*, [unpublished typescript in WSHC]

Rogers, K, 1984, *The Book of Trowbridge*, Barracuda Books

Smart, T W Wake, 1841, *A Chronicle of Cranborne and the Cranborne Chase*, Nichols & Son

Smith, L T (ed), 1907, *The Itinerary of John Leland ...*, George Bell & Sons

Straton, C R (ed), 1909, *Survey of the lands of William First Earl of Pembroke*, Roxburgh Club

Tatton-Brown, T, Reconstructing the medieval landscape around Salisbury, *Sarum Chronicle 9,* 2009, 30-36

VCH *Wilts* 3

VCH *Wilts* 4

VCH *Wilts* 5

VCH *Wilts* 6

Webb, S and B, *1913, English Local Government: The Story of the King's Highway,* Longmans, Green & Co

Wordsworth, C (ed), 1902, *The Fifteenth Century Cartulary of St. Nicholas, Salisbury, with other records,* Brown & Co

In WSA at the WSHC

492/239, Copy of a grant by letters patent to Sir William Herbert, of various property including the tolls of Harnham Bridge. 1547

1672/39, Rev Edward Hickman's records of St Nicholas Hospital, Sarum, pt 1, 1711, pt 2, 1712-13

2057/A1/1, Pembroke estate account book. 1562

A1/110/1810E, Wiltshire Quarter Sessions. Great Roll, Easter Session. 1810

A1/160/1, Wiltshire Quarter Sessions Order book. 1642-54

A1/160/2, Wiltshire Quarter Sessions Order book. 1653-68

A1/531/23/5, Wiltshire Quarter Sessions. Schedules of county bridges. 1859-61

A1/531/8/1, Wiltshire Quarter Sessions. Plans, contracts, agreements etc concerning repair, rebuilding or widening of county bridges, Harnham. 1774

A1/533/2/3, Wiltshire Quarter Sessions. Plan and elevations of county bridges. *c*1877

F1/100/6/7, Wiltshire County Council, Roads and Bridges Committee Minutes. 1921-25

F2/250/71, Wiltshire County Council. Correspondence relating to purchase of stone depot from Salisbury Corporation and repair of Harnham Bridge. 1890-1907

G23/132/17, Salisbury City Council. Correspondence relating to Harnham Bridge Rebuilding. 1929-34

G25/1/179 Wilton Borough Council. Authority by mayor to three people to demand customs and tolls of passengers over Harnham Bridge. 1682

Notes

1   WSHC 1672/39

2   The date is from Bingham's ordination of June 1244 respecting the bridge, which refers to the bridge and chapel as new (*novi pontis et capelle*): Benson and Hatcher, 732

3   *Cal Pat* 1413-16, 161; Davies, vol 2, 8, 212, 214

4   Gelling and Cole, 94-5

5   E Ledwich, *Antiquitates Sarisburienses*, 1771, 90-1. This cannot be the Cow Lane shown on Donn's 1797 map of Salisbury as part of the present Salt Lane. Ledwich said that it ran down the back of Dr Baker's house, which is believed to have been in St Ann Street.

6   Benson and Hatcher, 95-6

7   *Placita de quo Warranto* (Record Commisioners), 185; *VCH Wilts* vol 4, 458

8   WSHC 1672/39, 85

9   Harrison, 68, 70

10   Rogers, 11-12

11   The location and importance of Britford and Longford are discussed by T Tatton-Brown 'Reconstructing the medieval landscape around Salisbury, *Sarum Chronicle* 9, 2009, 30-36 (on 31)

12   Coates, 78. Recorded in Domesday, it means 'bridge of the dwellers at Ford' – the name of the place before there was a bridge.

13   Tim Tatton-Brown pers comm

14   *Cal Pat* 1413-16, 161; the text is given in full in Wordsworth, 162-3: pons, iuxta Hospitale sancti Nicholai ... Ayleswaterbrigg vulgariter nuncupatus.

15   Wordsworth, 28

16   Wordsworth, 118 (in 1393), 127 (in 1438-9); cf Davies, 245-6.

17   Chandler (2007), 56-63; Chandler (2004), 22-30

18   Smith, vol 1, 260, 262

19   VCH *Wilts* 6, 15; Chandler (1987), 13-14

20   Harrison, *Bridges*, 44, 58

21   The width is comparable with other major medieval town bridges: information from David Harrison

22   Dimensions from the 1933 booklet in WSA G23/132/17, which seems to have resulted from a more detailed measurement than the summary in RCHM(E) (1980), 51. Leland (note 15 above) claimed the northern bridge had four arches; cf Price, F, 1753, *Observations on the Cathedral Church of Salisbury*, 29-30.

23   Price, 29; cf Duke, 514-16. Harrison, *Bridges*, 122, notes a similar theory for the construction of Bristol Bridge, but comments: 'This is the stuff of legend'. Price may in fact have been familiar with Leon Batisti Alberti's *Ten Books of Architecture*, first published in English translation in 1726, which told of a bridge built in antiquity by these means across the Nile (1755 edition, 77)

24   Jones & Macray, 290-3

25   WSA 1672/39 (Hickman's notes) pt 2, 18-19; cf VCH *Wilts* 3, 344-5

26   Wordsworth, 241

27   Harrison, 200-1

28   Wordsworth, xlvi

29   Wordsworth, 33, 241

30   Jervoise, 73

31   Benson and Hatcher, 95

32   Flower, vol 2, 233-8

33   Summarised in *Cal Pat* 1413-16, 161; full transcript in Wordsworth, 162-3

34   VCH *Wilts* vol 6, 9

35   WSA 492/239

36   WSA 2057/A1/1

37   Straton, 200, 204: 'Maior et Burgenses Wiltonie pro tholneto, custumiis et aliis prodicuis pontis vocati Harneham Bridge sic olim dimissis ad firmam xxs.'

38   *Rotuli Hundredorum* (Record Commissioners), vol 2, 571 (the text is incomplete but the meaning seems clear). I am grateful to David Harrison for pointing out this reference.

39   WSHC 1672/39, p .2, 102

40   Harris, ii; Harris's source may have been Ledwich, *Antiquitates Sarisburienses*, 91.

41   WSHC G25/1/179

42   *VCH Wilts* vol 4, 458-9

43   Salisbury complained in 1275: *Rotuli Hundredorum*, vol 2, 267. That Wilton did not complain in similar fashion (vol. 2, 266-9, 280-1) may suggest that the toll was not then levied on Bulbridge.

44   Smart, 133-5; Dryden, A, 1906 *Memorials of old Wiltshire*, 88

45   Smart, *ibid*, quotes an example as late as 1710. See, picture p21 above.

46   *Hants Advertiser* 7 Oct 1848, 'Rambles in south Wiltshire'

47   Discussion in Harrison, 213-17

48   Johnson, *passim*

49   Riley, *passim*. Harnham Bridge was presented on no fewer than 24 occasions.

50   WSA 1672/39, pt.2, 101-2

51   *Calendar SPD Charles I*, 1636-7, 488; Cunnington, 115; Cockburn, 104-5

52   WSA 1672/39, pt 2, 113-15

53   WSA A1/160/1, sv Hilary 17 Charles I

54   WSA 1672/39, pt 2, 157

55   WSA A1/160/1, sv Easter 1652, Easter 1653; WSA A1/160/2, sv Hilary 1660/1; cfVCH *Wilts* vol 5, 107

56   All from WSA 1672/39 (Hickman), pt 2, 116-17

57   *HMC Var Col.* 1, 150

58   Goldney, 234.

59   WSA 1672/39, pt 2, 10. In 1703 the Chippenham overseers noted that Thomas Crook had been paid to repair 'Haringham' Bridge: *WANHM* 1933 vol 46, 328.

60   Webb, S and B, 89

61   WSA A1/531/23/5

62   eg *Whitehall Evening Post* 8019, 5-7 April 1798. Most details in this para from VCH *Wilts* vol 4, 256-70; see also Andrews and Dury, *Map of Wiltshire*, 1773.

63 It does not appear on East Harnham inclosure map: information from Tim Tatton-Brown.

64 This para: WSA A/531/8/1.

65 Price, 29-30

66 WSA A1/110/1810E, bundle relating to Harnham Bridge

67 Cowan, WRS 50, ix, xii, xiv

68 WSA A1/531/23/5

69 Howells and Newman (2011), WRS 64, 36-7

70 *Ibid*, 2-5

71 Trollope, A, *Autobiography*, 1883, 95-6 (1950 edition), cited by G Ridden, 'Trollope, Salisbury, and Winchester', *Hatcher Review* vol 3 (27), 1989, 330-6.

72 WSA A1/533/2/3, f 109

73 VCH *Wilts* vol 6, map on 71. See also below chapter 9, Wilcockson

74 WSA F2/250/71

75 This para: WSA F1/100/6/7 *passim*

76 This para: WSA G23/132/17, especially the souvenir booklet for the opening ceremony

77 *OED*; an earlier term was rond-point, used in London in 1903

78 WSA G23/132/17; Gover, 222

79 I am extremely grateful to David Harrison and Tim Tatton-Brown who read a draft of this paper and made many helpful suggestions and corrections. My thanks also to Steven Hobbs, Helen Taylor and their colleagues at the Wiltshire and Swindon History Centre for their interest and help; and to Wiltshire Council for permission to reproduce documents and maps in their possession. The remaining shortcomings are my own.

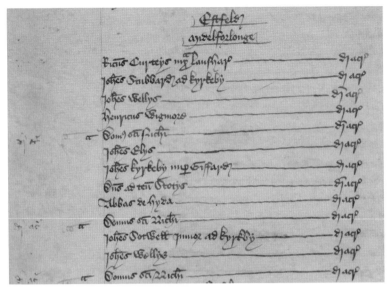

Extract from 1438 survey listing tenants of half-acre strips in Middle Furlong of the East Field. WSA 1672/46

Estfeld
Midelforlonge

Richardus Curteys, iuxta lanshar'	Dimidiam acram
Johannes Stubbard, ad Kyrkeby	Dimidiam acram
Johannes Wellys	Dimidiam acram
Henricus Wigmore	Dimidiam acram
¶Domus sancti Nicholai	Dimidiam acram
Johannes Elys	Dimidiam acram
Johannes Kyrkeby, nuper Giffard	Dimidiam acram
Dominus, ad tenementum Stotys	Dimidiam acram
Abbas de Hyda	Dimidiam acram
¶Domus sancti Nicholai	Dimidiam acram
Johannes Sotwell junior, ad Kyrkeby	Dimidiam acram
Johannes Wellys	Dimidiam acram
¶Domus sancti Nicholai	Dimidiam acram

Transcript of above

Estfeld
Midelforlonge

Richard Curteys by lanshar'	Half acre
John Stubbard near Kyrkeby	Half acre
John Wellys	Half acre
Henry Wigmore	Half acre
The house of St Nicholas (hospital)	Half acre
John Elys	Half acre
John Kyrkeby formerly Giffard	Half acre
The same towards Stotys tenement	Half acre
The Abbot of Hyde	Half acre
The house of St Nicholas (hospital)	Half acre
John Sotwell the younger near Kyrkeby	Half acre
John Wellys	Half acre
The house of St Nicholas (hospital)	Half acre

Translation of above

5 'The Fields Beneath': a glimpse of East Harnham in the middle ages

Steven Hobbs

The manor and tithing of East Harnham,[1] lay in the parish of Britford before administrative changes between 1854 and 1904 promoted it first to a separate ecclesiastical parish before it was subsumed by the urban sprawl of Salisbury as it spread over the banks of the rivers Avon and Nadder. Square shaped with an arm running eastwards along the Avon, the land rises from 150ft above sea level in the valley, through 178ft in the village to 300ft on its southern boundary. The soils are chalk and gravel and the sub soil chalk. In 1899 it comprised 362 acres.

Before much of East Harnham disappeared under tarmac and brick, it displayed all the characteristics of a chalk valley manor, with river valley water meadows, arable fields on the lower downs, and upper downs given over to sheep pasture. There are relatively few extant archives documenting its history. However, two important sources survive for its tenurial and topographical history in the Middle Ages: The 15th century cartularies of the Tropenell family and of the Hospital of St Nicholas.[2] Although cartularies had a fairly specific purpose to document the acquisition and ownership of lands and privileges 'as evidence of personal or corporate rights', it is possible to discern differences of emphasis in the interests of their lay and corporate owners.[3] Thomas Tropenell was a shrewd and ambitious lawyer, who amassed an impressive portfolio of manors and estates in Wiltshire as he sought to establish his family's power and prestige. His cartulary includes 125 deeds concerning the title to the manor of East Harnham, and estates within it, together with a detailed account of the owners of the manor. The impression is given that Tropenell's interest lay in the ownership of the manor, rather than the *minutiae* of its day to day management. The cartulary of St Nicholas' Hospital includes 25 deeds relating to the hospital's lands and, significantly, two detailed surveys of the manor, which suggest a more intimate association with the land.

These surveys provide a glimpse of the physical appearance of the manor which reveals the typical and familiar arrangement of strips in furlongs scattered among the open arable fields. Although the hospital never held the lordship, and remained one of a group of landholders within the manor, the surveys were a useful ready-made record of its holdings alongside other estates in East Harnham. As was commonly the case the positions of their strips in the common fields are described by the holders of adjoining strips, who appear to have been landowners and peasantry, here the customary tenants. Causepe, Calne, Harnham and Creklade were of the same families of grantees of freehold properties in the Tropenell cartulary.[4] St Nicholas' Hospital, De Vaux College and Hyde Abbey, probably held their lands in free alms and were thus largely exempt from seigneurial obligation and control.

The earlier survey, made in 1393, is titled (translated from the Latin): Concerning the lands of Thomas Lynford, which pertain to his lordship (*dominico suo*)... Lynford was lord of the manor of East Harnham until 1421.[5] It describes eight tenements, probably customary holdings, the occupiers of which owed labour services and other obligations to the lord. The lands are dispersed in the furlongs of the three open arable fields of the manor, East, Middle and West, together with small pieces of meadow. The tenements have one or two houses each which are described as being in the East field; clearly this was not the case, although it indicates that the proximity of this field to the village. They comprised about 12 acres, which represents a half virgate, the phrase used to describe the tenement of John atte More, a free tenant. Each tenant had the right to an amount of hay cut in the meadow of Homington. This is not mentioned in the later survey, and is a rather surprising perquisite since Harnham was particularly well endowed with meadowland.[6] Meadow land in Homington called Cawdon on the inclosure map of 1787 may reflect a common right that belonged to manors in the hundred of Cawdon.[7]

Three tenements are known by the names of former occupiers, probably tenants at the last time a survey was drawn up. This is a possible indicator of the lasting impact of the depopulation caused by the Black Death, either in the number of unoccupied holdings or the arrival of new men not sufficiently well established yet to impose their identities on the estates. Of these the one described as 'Formerly Thomas le lymbrenner' provides evidence of the production of lime, an important constituent in mortar, from the chalk bedrock. Building work in Salisbury meant that there was a constant demand for this locally-sourced commodity. A deed of 1302 in the Tropenell cartulary records the land of Edith widow la Lymberners, adjoining an acre conveyed in the document, which consolidates the history of this industry in the area.[8] One of the estates was described as being at Fordewey, and two others as occupied by Robert Fordewey and formerly John Fordewey which must refer to the crossing of the Avon which was superseded by the construction of Alylesward (Harnham) bridge in 1244.[9]

The survey is a rich source for topographical detail. In or adjoining the East Field interesting names include: Henway, Odstokcross, and the bothy between the bounds of East Harnham and Britford. For Middle field we find; the Buttes, and a lime pit at Brodhull; Cerdlond or Cardeland. West field offers; above holwey, near the field of West Harnham; a road called le Siche[10]; above the cleeves; above the ditch; Harnhamcrosse; the road called Harnham Hill; Personnes gate near the field of West Harnham. Meadows include; tethyngeswathe, le Fordweye; the ditch between the meadow of East and West Harnham.

The later survey (1439) is arranged quite differently from its predecessor and appears to cover all the land in the open fields and meadows, in total about 325 acres. Two estates, called the new tenement and Stotys or Stokys tenement, each comprising about 15 acres, may be customary estates. It is unclear whether the other six estates described in 1393 had been dispersed and these remaining two were kept in hand and leased out. East and Middle fields appear to have been conflated, whether this reflects the position on the ground or a scribal error is unclear, although it is not uncommon for fields to be merged especially as greater importance may have been put on the furlongs as a means of identification. The survey has a puzzling title which literally translated from the Latin reads 'A new terrier comprising [*continens*] how the lands and meadows of each [*de utraque*] Harnham are held and lie in diverse parts and the names of those who hold them, 17 Henry VI' [1438]. This implies that land in East and West Harnham is included. However, having only covered some pasture and arable land in one furlong in the East field, it then begins again under the title East Harnham Lands and meadows there ... 16 Sep 1439.

Nevertheless there appears to have been some uncertainty about the lands covered in the survey. An annotation in an early 17th century hand on the first page of the section of West Field describes West field as being in West Harnham, although it is clearly the same field as described in 1393. The error probably arose in the appearance of West Harnham in the descriptions of furlongs in West Field abutting the border between the manors; thus by le Lansher[11] of West Harnham by the highway leading to Shaftesbury (probably the road referred to as the way of Whitshit by Knyllforlang).[12] The original rubric of the survey describes the meadow lands in two sections East Harnham, on the side bank of the river, opposite the wall of the cathedral close beside Shortforlang, and West Harnham, Long furlong beside the hedge (*sepem*), down to the river below the cathedral close, and may explain the title of the unfinished survey of 1438. However, the occupiers are the same in both sections, suggesting that East Harnham tenants enjoyed rights in the meadows of West Harnham.

The survey also contains topographical detail. The Buttes, in Middle field in 1393, are described in 1439 as being on the N and S sides of the lime pit; there is a furlong called shorte buttes below the hill beside the lime pit. Knyllforlang is described as being on W side of the lime pits; and a lime kiln (*puteum calceti*) in West Field is described as being near the highway called Whitwey.

Although the documentary evidence does not allow the location of the common fields to be determined with any real precision, nevertheless the Britford tithe apportionment, 1840, and Britford inclosure award, 1847, offer some clues.[13] The inclosure award is particularly significant as it gives the boundaries of the tithing of East Harnham, which probably reflects the extent of the medieval manor. 218 acres (covering the tithing south of the village) which were enclosed under this award weredescribed as arable in the tithe apportionment.

In 1840 the land immediately south of the A354 as it joins the road to Odstock is called Upper and Lower Woodborough Piece(s). The field on the east side of these is Bouchers Piece but Lime Kiln Hedge furlong in the inclosure award, a name which provides evidence of the vestigial medieval field system.

The North part of the tithing, running down to the river Avon comprised 115 acres of meadow and water meadow in 1840. It is easy to imagine that the three open fields being bisected by the road known as Harnham Hill and the present A354. However, it was not as straightforward as this; a small enclosure in the inclosure award called East field straddles as it joins the road to Odstock. Furthermore the proximity of the East field to the village, indicated in the 1393 survey is emphasised in 1439 by references to a ham in the East field by the end of the bridge now built (*modo hedificat*), and land down to the water by the way to the marsh, which suggest that the field wrapped itself around the village and across the present A36.

The derivation of the name of the land immediately south of the village, called the Cliff on the OS 6in (1889), is probably due to the extraction of chalk from the pit described in the inclosure award as the old chalk pit.

These aspects of the history of the manor owe much to the assiduousness of two masters of St Nicholas' Hospital: Nicholas Upton, who realised the usefulness of the surveys in managing the hospital's estates and ensured their preservation in the cartulary which was compiled probably during his term of office around 1450, and Christopher Wordsworth, who appreciated their historical significance, and published them in his edition of the cartulary and history of the hospital about 450 years later. Both have served historians of East Harnham very well.

Bibliography

Davies, J S, (ed), 1908, *The Tropenell Cartulary: being the contents of an old Wiltshire muniment chest,* 2 volumes, WANHS

Davis, G R C, 2010, *The Medieval Cartularies of Great Britain, xiv,* revised edition, British Library

VCH *Wilts* 6

Wordsworth, C, (ed) 1902, *The Fifteenth Century Cartulary of St Nicholas'
Hospital, Salisbury with other records*, from a transcript by T H Baker of
Mere

Notes

1   The title is borrowed from Gillian Tyndall's history of Kentish Town,
republished Phoenix Press, 2002. The author is grateful to John Hare
for his comments on a draft of this article.

2   Davies – the original remains at Great Chalfield, near Trowbridge, the
Tropenell house where it was compiled. Wordsworth – the original is in
the hospital's archive at Wiltshire and Swindon History Centre (WSA
1672/46).

3   Davis, (2010)

4   Davies, vol 2, pp 172-255.

5   Lynford was succeeded by John atte Borgh who conveyed the manor
to Walter lord Hungerford in 1442. Davies, vol 2, pp 215-217.

6   Vestiges of this are found in the inclosure award of East Harnham with
a grant of about 1 acre in Homington parish meadow (1847; EA);
similar rights are found in the inclosure awards for Odstock (1787;
EA28) , and Coombe Bissett (1806; EA106).

7   WSA EA 26.

8   Davies, vol 2, p 224.

9   VCH *Wilts* 6, 88 the bridge replaced a ford in 1244. See above chapter
4, Chandler

10 *siche* is the OE for a stream in marshland, and so is not an obvious
location for the name in this case. Its derivation here is unclear.

11 ie lanchard, an unploughed division between two pieces of arable land.

12 Whitesheet hill about 13 miles west of Harnham on the old road to
Shaftesbury which ran along the edge of the race course.

13 WSA TA/Britford; EA166.

6 Harnham's Mills

Kenneth Rogers

West Harnham parish contained three mills – what is now known as Harnham Mill, the mill on the northern edge known as Fisherton, and the one in the north-west, known as Bemerton. Over the years there has been some confusion in interpreting sources describing these, particularly Harnham and Bemerton Mills.

In the accounts that follow material at the Wiltshire and Swindon History Centre has been used that was not available in the 1950s when the Harnham Women's Institute researched their history of the village (published 1954), nor indeed when

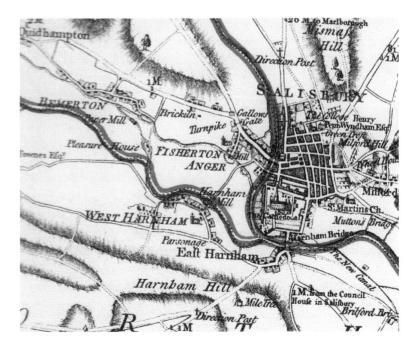

etail from Andrews'
d Dury's map of
iltshire 1773, WRS
68

the economic history volume of Wiltshire's *Victoria County History* (published 1959) was written. The section of that work on 'The paper-mills' refers to West Harnham throughout the relevant paragraph, although meaning Bemerton as stated in the first sentence.[1] RCHM(E)'s entry on Harnham Mill references this page of *VCH* 4, and then says certain construction details 'may suggest that the building was designed primarily for paper-making.[2] As will be shown, the histories of Bemerton, Harnham and Fisherton mills are closely linked.

The paper mill at Bemerton

A book produced by Wynkyn de Worde, the early English printer, in 1485, contains the statement that the paper it was printed on was made in England by John Tate. Henry VII visited Tate's mill, somewhere near Hertford, in 1498, but the enterprise appears to have ended before Tate made his will in 1507. An early tract on economic matters, John Hales's *Discourse of the Common Weal*, refers to Tate's production of paper, but says that at the time of writing, about 1549, no paper was made in the country, so that England had to depend on imports.

There appears to have been a paper mill at Fen Ditton near Cambridge by 1557, and the same mill was still in use in 1599, though the working may not have been continuous.[3] At roughly the same period, the 1550s or 1560s, a paper mill was established at Bemerton. The evidence comes from two statements by John Aubrey. In his *Natural History of Wiltshire* he wrote:

> At Bemarton near Salisbury is a paper mill, which is now, 1684, about 130 years standing and the first that was erected in this county; and the workmen there told me, 1669, that it was the second paper mill in England.[4]

Elsewhere in his notes Aubrey repeated the statement about it being the second mill in England, but there he said that it was of 112 years' standing in 1681.[5] He thus gives us two possible starting dates for Bemerton, 1554 and 1569.

Andrews and Dury's Map of Wiltshire of 1773 marks a Paper Mill very close to Bemerton, as does Greenwood's of 1820. The more detailed map attached to the West Harnham Inclosure Award of 1787 shows that the mill was actually just inside that parish.[6] Although it is not marked as a paper mill on that map, the ownership of John Baker, and a copy of part of the map on to a later deed, make it certain that this mill is the paper mill called Bemerton Mill in a series of deeds to be quoted shortly.

Our first information about the ownership of the mill comes from a deed of 1700 by which William Turner of Bemerton, gentleman, son and heir of William Turner late of the Close of Sarum, deceased, mortgaged the reversion of it (which means that it was let on lease) for £500 to Richard Long of Salisbury. The property was described as a messuage in West Harnham and the paper mills with wheels, shafts, stocks, hammers, troughs, and all other things belonging to the milling or beating of stuff to make paper. Thomas Harward or Harwood is named as a former occupier. Although this deed does not refer specifically to the paper mill being the one near Bemerton, one of the small pieces of meadow belonging to it lay in Bemerton bounded on the south by the river running from the paper mills, which links it to this site.[7]

Deeds of another property in West Harnham show that William Turner the elder held the manor of West Harnham in right of his wife Mary, who had a son and heir, William Horne, by a former marriage to John Horne.[8] According to their monument in West Harnham church, she was 25 years older than Turner. The older William died in 1699, and his son, who must have been by a former marriage, died intestate in 1708.[9]

After 1700 there is a gap in our knowledge of the ownership of the mill until we come to a series of title deeds of Bemerton Mill in the Longford Castle collection at the Wiltshire and Swindon History Centre. These show that before 1763 the owner of the mill was Thomas Baker, who had carried on business as a clothier in New Street in Salisbury. By 1763 he had left off business, and he then settled his Salisbury house and the paper mill in West Harnham on his son John's marriage to Susanna Gannett of Blandford. John was a clothier too. By 1796 John and Susanna were both dead, and in that year their trustees sold the paper mill to the tenant, James Wilkison. [10]

We can now turn to the paper makers who actually used the mill, several of whom are mentioned as previous occupiers in the deeds. The earliest of these was John Spelt, described as a paper maker and yeoman in his will made in 1697.[11] He was the son of Henry Spelt, who was married at Fugglestone (the mother church of Bemerton) in 1612. John was baptized there in 1624, when his parents were described as of Bemerton and Henry is listed under Bemerton in the Protestation Return of 1641-2.[12] John's marriage has not been found. He had a child baptised at Fugglestone in 1655, and two baptised at Bemerton in 1665 and 1676, so he may well have been present when Aubrey visited the mill in 1669. John's probate inventory amounted to a modest £46 18s, and shows that he farmed on a small scale. There is no reference to paper in it.

The next named tenant, William Compton, made his will and died in 1715; there is no reference to his being a paper maker.[13] His will named both a wife and a sister called Jane or Jone – it is very badly written. One of these was almost certainly the Jane Compton who, according to a pedigree compiled in 1819, married the next occupant of the mill, George Thompson.[14] He insured his household goods and stock at his house and paper mills all under one roof at West Harnham in 1726, and took an apprentice to paper making in 1750. He died in 1753.[15]

George Thompson's only surviving child, Molly, married James Wilkison, who took apprentices to paper making between 1761 and 1777. A monument in Bemerton church to a child of his describes him as of the paper mills in 1779. His tenancy under John Baker is recorded in the land tax assessments from 1780 onwards, and, as we have seen, he bought the freehold of the mill in 1796.[16] By the time he made his will in 1809 the mill was occupied by his son-in-law, James Saunders, who had married Jane Wilkison in 1792. In 1811 Wilkison made a 99–year lease to Saunders at a rent of £25 15s 9d. Wilkison died in 1814, aged 77, and the ownership of the mill passed, as his will directed, to Saunders. He died in 1815, apparently without issue, and his executors sold the mill to James Wilkison Forward, who was the son of James Wilkison's other daughter, Sarah.

J W Forward was the last paper maker at Bemerton. He was still in business in 1830, and the mill was mentioned, as No 344, in the Excise List of 1832.[17] Early in 1836 it was offered for sale by auction, as the well-known premises called Bemerton Paper Mill, with the dwelling house. It was particularly suitable for a paper machine, or could be easily converted to a flour mill or for any manufactory requiring room and a powerful command of water. It must have failed to sell, and later in the year Forward and his mother released the freehold to the mortgagees. The whole property, including 15 acres of water meadow, was sold to Charles Finch, who owned the lunatic asylum in Fisherton. A further attempt to sell by auction was made in 1838.[18] Reporting a robbery at the mill in 1839, the *Wiltshire Independent* said that its working had been discontinued.[19] In 1840 the whole property was sold to Lord Radnor, and no more is known of the mill.

West Harnham Mill

In 1299 Richard Pinnock was paying rent for property in West Harnham which included two mills, one of which was a fulling mill.[20] One of the mills was at Bemerton, perhaps on the site of the later paper mill. Two men were involved in a theft from it in 1306.[21] It seems likely, however, that the fulling mill was at West Harnham. In 1386 a fulling mill described as being there was the property of John Pinnock, and it was still being held in trust for the family in 1424.[22]

An interesting transaction relating to cloth manufacture in the manor of West Harnham, though not specifically to a fulling mill, also comes from 1386; an annual rent from it included eight ells of woollen cloth payable at Christmas.[23]

The oldest part of the present mill on the site has been authoritatively dated at about 1500, but no further documentary evidence has so far been found until 1634, when William Self was a fuller of West Harnham.[24] In 1643 the inhabitants of West Harnham petitioned the justices in Quarter Sessions on behalf of Richard Bevys, a man of civil behaviour. He had recently come to live in a house near adjoining to the fulling mill there, 'where at least from time to time 30 or 40 men are set on work ... they have usually been supplied with bread, cheese, and drink for their relief and sustenance by such as formerly dwelt in the house…'.[25]

A series of title deeds of the mill begins with the will of Robert Croome of West Harnham, clothier, made in 1713, and proved early the next year. He left West Harnham mill to his kinsman William Croome, who lived with him, though the devise was to be invalid if William married Mary London. The proviso had the desired effect, and William married Mary Feltham, daughter of a Salisbury baker, later in 1714. In the marriage articles of that year, in a settlement of 1718, and in William's will made in 1745, he is described as a miller. The settlement shows that he lived in a house in West Harnham, but that the mill adjoining it was a fulling mill. It also tells us that Robert Croome had purchased the house and mill from William Turner, whom we have already met in the history of Bemerton Mill. The West Harnham mill was no doubt let to a specialist fuller, and the milling of corn done at Fisherton, as described below.[26]

William and Mary Croome left no issue, and the ownership of the mill passed, according to a provision in Robert Croome's will, to a relative, Robert Croome Aylesbury of Shennington, Gloucestershire, wool comber. In 1754 he sold it to Joseph Champion of Salisbury, clothier, who insured it for £200. In 1760 Champion's mortgagees sold it to Martin Neave of Salisbury, mealman, and Mary Croome released her life interest in a deed which mentions James Sammens as a former occupier. Neave died in 1788. After the death of his widow in 1799 the mill was put up for sale as a fulling mill of six stocks, now in full trade, but capable of considerable improvements for a manufactory. The tenant was Samuel Williams, mealman.[27]

Neaves's devisees sold the mill to William Havers of Salisbury. When he put it up for sale in 1810, the advertisement only referred to it as a fulling mill, let to Thomas Lucas. Lucas had probably been occupying the fulling mill since 1792, when he advertised for a foreman who thoroughly understood the fulling business in the Salisbury manufactory.[28] In 1811 the mill was sold to Stephen Bell and James Sutton, millers, who owned it until 1846.

Harnham Mill by Elizabeth Wickens. ©Salisbury & South Wiltshire Museum

Although the actual owners of West Harnham Mill were millers, as was the lessee c1791-99, Samuel Williams, it is clear that the mill was used in the cloth trade. The deed of sale by Havers in 1811 included a newly erected mill on the site of an ancient leather mill occupied by Alexander Minty. He was a clothier of some years' standing; in 1794 the end of a partnership between him and another clothier was advertised.[29]

In 1813, when Bell and Sutton made a lease of the whole mill to Minty, it was described as a tucking mill with fulling stocks and other machinery late and for many years past occupied by Thomas Lucas, tucker.

The 1813 lease also reserved a part of the mill occupied by a clothier named Bachelor. This was John Bachelor whose machinery here and at Salisbury was for sale in 1818.[30] It included a scribbling engine, two carding engines, two billeys, and nine jennies. If, as is implied by the 1811 deed, Minty occupied the new building, Bachelor must have had his machinery in the old mill.

Minty was described as a clothier in successive directories until 1842. In 1838 he employed 15 hands at West Harnham, and in 1844, when an offence against the Factory Acts was committed there, it was described as a yarn factory occupied by Alexander Minty of Salisbury, yarn factor. This was evidently the new part, for in a valuation of the parish in 1840 the old mill was in use as a bone mill. A sale particular of 1848 described it as a fulling or bone mill with two wheels – but by now Salisbury was producing no cloth to be fulled. The new building was then empty.[31]

The later history of the West Harnham mill site as a bone mill, a candle factory, and a hotel, is told in Michael Cowan's 2007 book, which describes the buildings in detail.

Fisherton Mill

A few references to a mill in Fisherton from 1086 onwards are given in *VCH Wilts 6*. The detailed history of the mill begins in 1653 with a deed which states that there had been disputes about the inheritance of the lord of the manor, George Lowe, which had gone to the arbitration of Robert Hyde and Walter Norborne. In pursuance of their award, Richard Lowe of Plumley, Hampshire, conveyed three water grist mills under one roof and a house adjoining to Matthew Raymond of Puckshipton in

Beechingstoke.[32] This no doubt marks the separation of the mill from the manor. After this there is gap until the early 18th century, when it was owned by Robert Croome. From him the sequence of ownership was exactly the same as that of West Harnham Mill described above until 1846.[33]

The settlement of 1718 mentions John Bolten and Thomas Battin as former occupiers, no doubt during the Turner ownership, and describes the premises as two water grist mills, one malt mill, and one oatmeal mill. In view of the descriptions of successive owners as millers or mealmen, it is clear that the major part of Fisherton Mill was used in this trade continuously. But there was plenty of water power, and in 1762 the mill was extended to accommodate a new trade of leather dressing. This would have used stocks very similar to those used for fulling. In 1762 a journeyman fellmonger who could pare and grind was wanted at the newly erected leather mills in Fisherton, where pelts and skins of all kinds were bought. The name of the leather dresser was John Mildred, who advertised in 1763 that he could supply glovers, breeches makers, and shopkeepers with rough and grounded shammy leathers and buck, doe, and taw leather.[34]

No further reference to this trade on the site has been found, and when the property was advertised in 1799 it was described as a modern handsome house and flour mills with two wheels and three pairs of stones and bolting mills capable of twenty loads of corn a week. The occupier was Samuel Williams, mealman.[35]

Fisherton Mill with workmen. ©Salisbury & South Wiltshire Museum

However, in 1803 the new owner, William Havers, described as a miller, let a corn mill, part of Fisherton Mill, to Thomas Webb, a Salisbury baker, for seven years.

The part used as a leather mill was probably later used in the cloth trade. A mortgage of 1823 includes Fisherton Mill and a mill adjoining of three floors 60 feet by 18 feet, sometime since used for machinery in the woollen manufacture by Alexander Minty. As we have seen, Minty was in business in the 1790s, before which little machinery was used. The same building can be recognized in the 1848 sale particulars as a three floor mill adjoining Fisherton Mill, used for the pearling and grinding of barley.

In 1846 Bell and Sutton conveyed the Harnham and Fisherton mills to the mortgagee, the Salisbury banker W B Brodie. At that time both mills were occupied by George Gregory, who bought them when Brodie went bankrupt in 1848. George Gregory and then H G Gregory remained in business as millers and corn factors at Fisherton until 1899.[36] The sale catalogue shows that in 1891 the mill had been fitted with a 2 ½ sack roller plant with wheat cleaning machinery by Robinsons of Rochdale. It had a modern breast-shot wheel 12 ft 3 in wide and 12 ft in diameter, with 30 curved buckets. The barley mill adjoining had a wooden wheel which drove two pairs of stones and a bean crusher.[37]

The mill was sold to Edward Francis Bowle, who continued in business until 1931. He then sold to James Henry Bartlett of New Mills, Tisbury, who carried on business at both mills until 1953. The mills were then sold to H R and S Sainsbury, agricultural merchants and millers of Trowbridge, who also had mills there and at Quemerford near Calne, Chippenham, and Avonmouth. The end for Fisherton Mill came in 1969, when a compulsory purchase order was placed on part of the building to enable the road to be widened, and the mill was demolished, a sorry loss to the city of an exceptionally attractive group of buildings.[38]

In conclusion, there remains the question whether Harnham Mill, even for a short time, was used for making paper or was it always a fulling mill? My own research indicates that it was the latter continuously from the middle ages until the final collapse of the Salisbury woollen industry in the first half of the 19th century.[39] When John Aubrey spoke of the paper mill at Bemerton did he really mean West Harnham? Would he have failed to mention one at West Harnham, equally old or older, if there had been one there? Would the petitioners of 1643 have failed to mention the presence of a paper mill, which would have added weight to their case?

Bibliography

Aubrey, J, (originally published 1847) 1969, *Natural History of Wilts*, David & Charles

Aubrey, J, 1898, *Brief Lives*, Clarendon Press, vol 2

Coleman, D C, 1958, *The British Paper Industry 1495-1860*, Clarendon Press

Fry, E A, 1911-13, Wiltshire Protestation Return of 1641-2, *Wilts Notes and Queries*, vol 7, p16-21, 162-7

Kirby J J, (ed),1986, *Abstracts of fleet of fines relating to Wiltshire 1377–1509*, WRS vol 41

Pugh R B (ed), 1978, *Wiltshire gaol delivery and trailbaston trials 1275-1306*, WRS vol 33

Rogers, K H, 1976, *Wiltshire and Somerset Woollen Mills*, Pasold Research Fund

RCHM(E), 1980, *Salisbury* Vol 1

VCH *Wilts* 4

WSA at the WSHC:

EA 27, West Harnham Inclosure Award, 1787

Fugglestone and Bemerton Parish Registers

P5/1709/54, Administration bond of William Turner, West Harnham. 1709

P2/S/1043, Inventory and will of John Spelt, yeoman and paper maker, Fugglestone St Peter. 1698

P5/15Reg/328B, Will of William Compton, West Harnham. 1715

P8/43, Administration bond, George Thompson, junior, West Harnham. 1757

130/4, Lease of crown lands in the manor of E Harnham, 1596; Deeds of land in the manors of E and W Harnham, 1699-1737; Lease of land in manor of W Harnham, 1818

451/511, Deeds relating to the manor and farm of W Harnham; to E Harnham farm and to yearly cut of grass from the latter; to tithes of Netherhampton; brief and order on issue of lease of property in manor of W Harnham. 1695-1795

490/396, Deeds, wills and abstracts of titles relating to paper mill at W Harnham known as Bemerton Mill, lands in Harnham and Bemerton and cottages in Bemerton. 1763-1840

529/177, Miscellaneous letters and papers including pedigree of the Thompson family of Bemerton paper mill. 19th century

715/2, Deeds and papers relating to Fisherton Mill House and site of mill etc. 1931-72

727/8/19, Sale particulars 1838 of Bemerton Paper Mills... and deed of land. 1786-1838

776/515, Bundle of 25 deeds of the manor of Fisherton Anger, property in Fisherton Anger and W Harnham, including the capital messuage of Fisherton Anger, three water grist mills, the advowson of Fisherton Anger church and houses and land. 1589-1680

1214/86, Deeds of Fisherton Anger corn mill; land in Fisherton Anger; W Harnham Mill. 1859-1871

G23/150/47, Salisbury City Council records, deeds of water, corn and fulling mills called Fisherton Mills, houses and lands in W Harnham and Fisherton Anger, and W Harnham Mills (with sale particulars, 1848). 1713-1855

G23/150/94, Salisbury City Council records, deeds of assorted properties including land and fulling-mill in W Harnham. 1270-1430

A1/345/200 Land Tax assessments, West Harnham 1781-1830

A1/110 Quarter Sessions Great Roll, Hilary 1634

Notes

1   VCH *Wilts* 4, 245
2   RCHM(E), 171-2
3   Coleman, 40-41
4   Aubrey, (reprinted 1969), 95
5   Aubrey, (1898) 323.
6   WSA EA 27
7   WSA 130/4
8   WSA 451/511
9   WSA P5/1709/54
10 WSA 490/396, used hereafter to the end of the account of Bemerton Mill
11 WSA P2/S/1043
12 Fugglestone and Bemerton Parish Register; *Wilts Notes and Queries* vii, 164
13 WSA P5/15Reg/328B
14 WSA 529/177
15 VCH *Wilts* 4, 245. WSA P8/43
16 WSA A1/345/200
17 VCH *Wilts* 4, 245
18 WSA 727/8/19; *SJ* 22 January 1838
19 *Wiltshire Independent* 11 April 1839
20 VCH *Wilts* 4, 119
21 Pugh (1978), 984
22 WSA G23/150/94
23 Kirby, 98
24 Marriage licence
25 WSA A1/110, Quarter Sessions Great Roll, Hilary 1634

26 WSA G23/150/47, used hereafter to the end of the account of Harnham Mill
27 *SJL* 20 May 1799
28 *ibid* 21 February 1792
29 *ibid* 17 March 1794
30 *ibid* 6 April 1818
31 Rogers (1976), 255
32 WSA 776/515
33 WSA G23/150/47, used hereafter to the end of the account of Fisherton Mill
34 *SJL* 28 June 1762, 3 January 1763
35 *ibid* 20 May 1799
36 WSA 1214/86
37 WANHS Library, Devizes, sale catalogue
38 WSA 715/2
39 Rogers (1976), 254-5

7 William Small's Harnham

Ruth Newman

Cockfighting and badger baiting at Harnham chalk pit, someone tossed by a wild cow on Ayleswade Bridge, tragic suicides and accidents, the value of boats on the River Avon, for both transporting windows and picking blackcurrants,

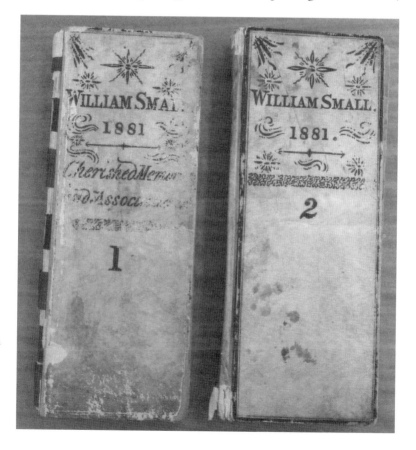

front covers of
two volumes, each
ntaining 368 pages,
William Small's
rished Memories
Associations. WSA
/2

Harnham Bridge, showing the Smalls' house and garden, left centre ©Salisbury & South Wiltshire Museum

Harnham Bridge, Salisbury.

prejudice suffered by early Methodists; these are just a few of the fascinating details revealed in William Small's *Cherished Memories and Associations.*[1]

This exciting memoir provides new information about 19th century Salisbury and Harnham. William Small (1820-1890) was a painter and glazier. He spent his whole life in the area, working with his brothers in the family firm that had been established when his father, also William, set up on his own. Writing in 1881 at 1, New Street (currently *The Wig and Quill*), he looked back over his life and that of his parents, the pages of his 'memories' revealing an unexpected level of literacy and breadth of reading. His colourful account of local society is from the perspective of a working man, recalling well-known buildings on which he was employed and amusing anecdotes from both his and his father's lifetimes. Such working class memoirs are extremely rare and give a unique glimpse of society in East Harnham in the early 19th century, a rural community, part of Britford until 1904, but within easy walking distance of the city. Victorian photographs show clusters of thatched cottages, with Ayleswade Bridge and William Small's house almost unchanged.

William Small was born on 16 May 1820 at East Harnham, the eldest child of William and Maria Small. The biographical details of his parents, beloved sister Henrietta and his own childhood give an insight into a respectable working family at this time. He appears to have enjoyed a contented, stable background; *'I turn my thoughts back to my childhood, and remember the happy season of Dear Parents, Pretty garden, & Boat's* (II, 137).

Of William and Maria's eight children, three died in infancy, Elizabeth only lived to the age of eleven, and the others – William, John, Henrietta and George all reached adulthood, the men living into old age (I, 66, II, 279). Elizabeth, who was just six years younger than William died quite suddenly in December 1837 in their house on Harnham Bridge and was given a walking funeral to Britford church. *'My father & mother was greatly affected at her death, (he) sat up with her for several nights following & said afterwards that he never felt so near another world as then'* (I, 70-71).

William's paternal grandmother Lydia was widowed when her husband Charles died (*c*1792) in Hindon *'in the small pox, when that diseace(sic) was raging there'*, and she moved to East Harnham in the early 1790s with her three sons, Charles, James, and William who was considerably younger than his brothers. James disappeared to the West Indies and Charles died in 1809 at the Battle of Talevera in Spain (I, 41-2).[2]

The reason given for Lydia moving to Salisbury was to be nearer to her family. A brother James was a verger of the cathedral living in the Close, and her brother in law, James Millett, was a school master in Fisherton. William senior was apprenticed to *his* son, another James, a painter and glazier. (I, 47-8) Thus in 1804 or 1805 he began working at the trade in which his three sons would follow him for a period of over 80 years. Meanwhile he

h register entry
he marriage of
iam Small's par-
Britford church
. WSA 1868/2

had courted Maria Alsford of Fisherton whom he married at Britford church in the autumn of 1819 (I, 53).

In 1823 the family moved from *'a lowly cottage'* in East Harnham, (near the current Harnham Lodge, on the corner of Ayleswade Road and Britford Lane West) to Harnham Bridge, within the Liberty of the Close. There they lived in the southern house of the pair on the western side of the road until June 1840. William was just nine years old when John Constable painted his house. Perhaps he even watched the artist at work? He certainly *'passed many happy hours'* growing up there, fishing in the Avon and enjoying his garden *'paradise'* (I, 63-4). It must also have been a period of sadness, because in those 17 years he lost *'a Grand-Mother, 3 brother's and sister's in Infancy, and a sister 11 years of age, and an apprentice'*. All were buried in one grave in Britford churchyard (II, 279).

A sample of Willia[m] Small's handwritin[g] from his 'Strange S[tages] in Life' (II, 279)

The Smalls then moved into Salisbury to a new property in Exeter Street, before transferring their business in February 1844 to the centre of the city in Queen Street. Just under eight years later, November 1851, the family moved to 1 New Street, the house where William senior, Maria and Henrietta were to die. William married Elizabeth Sutton in 1852 living first in Exeter Street and then Brown Street. Their only son, another William died aged 17 in 1870. After his wife's death in 1875 he moved back to the family home in New Street and was still there when he wrote his 'Memories'.

These volumes give us previously unknown details on East Harnham, as well as a wealth of information on Small's contemporaries in the village – friends, acquaintances and tradesmen. The latter reveal the variety of occupations: grocer's and blacksmith's shops, bootmakers and carpenters, Browns, the stone masons, a *'very ancient family in East Harnham'* (I, 100-101). James Saunders was engaged in rope and twine manufacture and *'had a rope walk* on *Harnham Bridge, the whole length of the Centre of the long garden there'* (I, 214).

William enjoys recollecting amusing episodes both from his own childhood and from his father's. The following, dating from 1802-3, was obviously a popular family story about his twelve year old father, concerning 'Madam Bower' who *'had ample means, & was a little deranged in her mind'* but ' *allways dressed elegantly in silk'* to go to market. *'She was very fond of My Father ...* (and) *'on a Market day, he was to walk before her with a long walking stick, to keep the Cattle away from her, and that was very necessary, especially in those rude days, but my Father once nearly lost his life, going over Harnham Bridge with her, a Wild Cow tossed him within an hairs breadth, almost over the Bridge'* (I, 44-5).

On another occasion he describes how, with his brother and a friend he was *'down the water in our Boat with a Gun, it was the winter time ... & we were just about to fire at a thrush in one of his trees'* when the Rev Hugh Stevens, chaplain of St Nicholas's Hospital, appeared *'with a double-barrell'd pistol in each hand ... & he said he would shoot us for destroying his singing birds, we were not far from the Bridge, & we were up very quickly & under the Bridge, frightened enough'* (I, 22-4). William's father was a member of the Volunteer Infantry and used *'to Shoot the Trout from the Bridge occasionally'* but on one occasion *'he left the Gun* [in the house] *with the charge but partly drawn'*. In a potentially tragic episode William writes of how he and his brother John used the gun to frighten their Grandmother *'children like, full of mischief, … snapped it several times and frightened her'*. Not content with this, John later *'snapped it again & the gun exploded & blew down a lot of the Ceiling'* (I, 71-2).

Life on the Bridge

William Small provides a colourful account of life, work and death on Harnham Bridge. As one of the main routes into Salisbury there was always a hive of activity and bustle which he witnessed: farmers on horseback en route to market, politicians, Methodist ministers, tradesmen and even a mad dog who attacked William Wooff junior who *'was oblig'd to have* [2 or 3 fingers] *amputated at once'* (I, 153-4)

Much of the Smalls' early work took place on the bridge where they had a workshop and his writing gives valuable detail of materials and methods used in their trade. He recalls with pleasure a job they did for Mr Brownjohn in New Street: *'all the sashes were Glaz'd on Harnham Bridge by me, with best Crown Glass'* (I, 38). Transporting glass, and windows, could be difficult, and some ingenuity was needed: *'we glaz'd the lights & took them in our Boat, to the meadow opposite, & then into the road, because we could not get them up the stairs on Harnham Bridge'* (I, 167). Apprentices for his father's business were hired locally. One was his close friend, William Wooff; another, Leonard Talbot was *'a Harnham lad & a very good apprentice.'* Mark Eminton, from the Lane, East Harnham, however, brought disgrace as he *'committed himself with a Nursemaid of Mr J Hussey of the Close when she was walking in Britford fields one dinner time …'* (I, 154-5).

William's memories of his early life are usually positive. Proud of the gardens on the bridge, both the Smalls and their neighbours in the adjoining house (and therefore adjoining garden) had productive and attractive grounds. Mr Hill *'was a good gardener, had plenty out of his garden for their use, Good potatoes, Cabbage, Onion, lettuce etc & plenty of fruit, he had a splendid Harbour Interwoven with White roses & honeysuckles facing that beautiful meadow on the other side of the stream'* (I, 75). As well as being a skilled gardener, Mr Hill *'did purchase a large Eel pot or Holly, every year & have a rope attached to it, and bait it with snails, & throw it into the water by the side of his garden in different places, & allways have plenty of Eels'* which were a significant source of food (I, 75-6).

Harnham

William said of their garden *'One might call it a little paradise'*. It was certainly generously provided with fruit: *'The Waters edge was, well planted with black currant trees, which were generally loaded with fruit, and we had to pick a great portion of them in a Boat. The apple trees, one or two of them hanging over the stream ... the old russet tree at the entrance to the Garden almost which had been standing there for generations, 200 Years at least, bearing splendid fine fruit, my mother putting them away in a large hamper for the winter, and then they were delicious, as many as five or six beautiful Cherry Trees, Planted by me when young… A grape tree ran all over the old south wall, bearing a good crop of black Grapes'.* They also had flowers: *'especially White Roses & Gillyflowers, we had a show of splendid double Gillyflowers, one year in particular, quite a grand sight from the Bridge from 1ft to 1ft 6 inches in length, & filling the air with delicious perfume'* (I, 63-4).[3]

Additional local information is included, about well recorded catastrophes such as the 1841 floods which had such disastrous consequences in the Shrewton and Tilshead area (I, 77-83). His comments on the *'great flood'* were related to his own personal experiences: *'we & Mr Hill had left the 2 houses on the Bridge ... & a good job for us that we did, about 5 or 6 months and both houses were unoccupied, at the time of the flood, or some of us no doubt would have been drowned ... it was on Saturday just about dusk on the 16 January 1841, that the waters came down, the whole of the Close was flooded, & men pushed about in Boats.'* He also referred to the flooding of Fisherton, Exeter Street, East and West Harnham (I, 77).

Living on the bridge William noted dramatic happenings which were forcefully imprinted in his mind on the sad occasions when searches had to be made for people who had fallen into the river or jumped from Harnham Bridge. He records three such tragedies. On one occasion a young apprentice was missing from Castle Street and *'the water was drawn off, as much as possible, & the streams dragged but without success. About 7 or 8 days, or it may be 9, one clear frosty morning My father Myself & our Apprentice went down the stream in our Boat in search, the stream was low & very clear; Just as we approached the division of the water, the original stream and the New Cut, at the point of the Island facing Harnham Bridge; The drowner for Mr Jervoise, named Broad, was in a flat bottom boat, with another man, in search also ... suddenly he called out here he is". We went with our Boat to the spot & saw the body lying in a deep hole, at the angle of the Island ... We carried it to the Swan Inn, at East Harnham, & had some refreshment'* (I, 103-4).[4]

Another anecdote concerned the Wooff family, long time residents of Harnham, Methodists and good friends of the Smalls. Richard Wooff senior *'came to live at the foot of the Bridge in 1830, or 1829 ... [he] had the front altered & a new Shop Window, put in, which remains to this day ... in 1845 Mr Murcell ... was in Charge of a Horse ... & the horse threw him over the front Pails* (at Mr Wooff's) *clean through, this shop window, head foremost, breaking away, Glass & wood work of sash, to the inside of the Shop, where Mr Wooff was at work. Without the slightest injury to him. more than the fright, he happened to have his hat on, & that saved his head ... he had a most miraculous escape'* (I, 105-6).

Leisure and recreation in Harnham

For the self-employed working man there was probably not a great deal of time left for leisure although twice William climbed the cathedral spire, once to the very top (I, 162-4). As the son of a skilled craftsman, he probably enjoyed a reasonable standard of living; there is no evidence of grinding poverty in his youth. He spent many hours both as a child and as a young man enjoying country pursuits, rowing his boat on the Avon, being *'very fond of fishing'* (I, 130). He inherited his love of fishing from his father who *'I have heard him say, caught a very fine Grayling once at Harnham when a little boy when fishing for minnows, with a crook'd pin'* (I, 99-100). William, as a lad, was sent home to the 'Bridge' to get some paint for his father, *'but my mind was more on fishing than on work, it was a splendid morning in May, & the Trout were then in their beauty.* He went into his garden and *'in less than five minutes had a beautiful Trout on my hook ... and I was away again to my father, all done in less than Half an Hour'* (I, 27).

There were equally fond recollections of times in his boat: with Mr and Mrs Bowns and a picnic of *'Beer, Tobacco & Bread & Cheese, & we used to take the Gun & shoot the rats etc'* (I, 214), William Small senior also used the opportunity to make a little extra cash from hiring out boats at East Harnham: *'[My father] thought he would get a Boat or two to let out by the hour, or by the day, for pleasure or fishing ... The young gentlemen from the Close & town soon paid visits* (the Eyres, Wyndhams, Bouveries, Husseys among others). *General Wyndham* (brother of Wadham Wyndham MP) came *'nearly every afternoon ... for to sail up & down the river ... even Noblemen used to come in the May month, for Trout Fishing*

... The Honbl Mr St John, one of the Bolingbroke family ... Used to come every year ... he used to kill the fine trout, with the Minnow from Harnham Bridge ... & I often used to attend him, & land his fish, he was very kind to me & used to give me as much as five shillings ... besides Hooks, Gut, sometimes a good line etc'. Apart from the not insubstantial payment, William shared the generous hamper sent from the *White Hart* (I, 61-2). It was not only the Salisbury gentry who made use of the boats but also *'Most of the Methodist club'* (I, 62, 73). The success of the boats had a profitable spin-off for his father's trade as *'these young Gentlemen, spoke a word for him at home & he soon began to work for their parents'* (I, 62-3).

Older forms of sport and rustic pursuits lingered on in the first half of the 19th century, as William notes. Before the house 'Harnham Cliff' was built in 1825, *'the Cliff ... was a wild, romantic, uncultivated place, a large chalk pit ...* (and according to his father) *'a secluded place, for all sorts of games, such as fighting ... cock fighting, badger baiting, Mountebanks, Snapping at treacle loaves, camping place for Gipsey's'* (I, 31-2,). William also records that he read in an old (1803) *Salisbury Journal* that the *Rose and Crown* was advertising cock fighting and badger baiting during the three days of the Salisbury Races (I, 100).[5]

Allotments were available for people who wanted to grow their own food. After recording the building of Harnham House for Mr W Brownjohn, William wrote that *'the other portion of the field was let out in allotments for the use of the inhabitants of Harnham, & so it is at this day, and new oak pegs that divided the allotments at each side of the centre path was painted white & numbered by my Father'* (I, 32).

Methodism in Harnham

For the Wesleyan historian the 'Memories' provide considerable information about the Harnham community of Methodists and their relationship with Salisbury. Despite receiving most commissions of work from Church of England employers, the Small family remained staunch Methodists and the chapel in St Edmund's church Street, Salisbury was central to William's upbringing. His mother, Maria, kept up family prayers while trying to instil the same fervour in her husband and children. Ministers from the city were frequent visitors to the Smalls' house on the bridge. There are also fascinating glimpses of the difficulties that Methodists faced in the early 19th century and the courage shown in the face of considerable harassment. His grandmother, Lydia, *'was a godly woman'* who held prayer meetings at her house, and she and others were taunted by mobs who *'would follow them up from Harnham with tin pots, kettles & frying pans & back again from the Chapel, (in St Edmund's Church Street) & no one to interfere, no policemen, no order, no nothing … the majority of the Harnham people was strongly against the Methodists'.*[6] He continues to record the physical problems endured by his father and friends, who when listening to the Sunday preaching in Harnham *'in a field down the old lane'* had to suffer the indignity of *'a booth erected there, for drinking & smoking & any sorts of Games to annoy them & … drive them away',* even threatening to shoot *'their dam'd Methodist hen'* which wandered into the gardens of *The Swan.* Despite the antagonism the *'band of Godly young men',* the Hardings, the Wooffs, the Miells and William Small senior, continued to hold their prayer meetings *'in their Houses & Singing & Godly exhortations, instead of drinking & dancing'* (I, 48-50).[7]

Houses

As craftsmen, the Smalls worked on several houses in Harnham, some of which no longer exist. Harnham Cliff, off the Old Blandford Road, was a substantial mansion and *'was built by the present Mr Kelseys Grand Father in 1825, Steward to the Earl of Radnor … I remember when in my fifth year, going with my Father there, … all the Doors inside, are made of solid Walnut'* (I,28). Mrs Denison, mother of Bishop Denison lived at the Cliff and the Smalls worked for her for several years before losing their work to Robert Mackrell, plumber of Blue Boar Row, Salisbury, who undercut them (I,143). A later occupant was Edward Everett, judge, who with his wife founded East Harnham School on land adjoining the churchyard.[8]

Harnham House was built as a property investment for William Brownjohn (*c*1782-1852), Salisbury auctioneer and valuer. Elected mayor in 1845 he was a great supporter of the Smalls. The house was constructed in 1831 *'on a part of the field to the left, as you ascend the lower Harnham Hill, leading to Downton … it was built by Mr Weavings of Exeter St. and my father did the Painting* (I, 32).[9]

Residents of Harnham House included Mrs Taunton, a

Harnham

arnham Cliff
ouse. AA69_02796.
Crown copyright.
nglish Heritage. This
otograph taken
ortly before demoli-
n, original build-
g is the right-hand
tion.

clergyman's widow from Stratford Tony who lived there before it was finished from 1832-3. She married the Rev George Lewes Benson and moved into 17 The Close in 1834. Later alterations were made to the house in about 1840 for the Rev John Coope when new bow windows were added to the ground floor rooms at the front. An intriguing character, '*he kept a lot of Dog's & Servants, and was very liberal at Christmas time, he invited the poor of Harnham, to a sumptuous repast, in the Coach House*'. Unfortunately his later history is controversial; he became a Roman Catholic, left Harnham for the King's House (currently the Salisbury and South Wiltshire Museum), made himself unpopular with both the Close residents and his employees, disappearing '*like a morning dream* [leaving] *some of the tradesmen in the lurch*' (I, 34-5).

Adjacent to Harnham House and still standing, is Harnham Lodge, with its cob walls and thatched roofs.[10] William Brownjohn rebuilt the cottage, and as a widower he passed his mayoralty there in 1845. He occupied the cottage until his death in 1852 (I, 37-8, II, 281-2).

Public Houses

The memoirs give us significant detail about the two public houses of East Harnham, *The Swan Inn* (currently *The Grey Fisher*), and *The Rose and Crown*. The latter, used as a school where the Small children attended was owned by the Browns (stonemasons) '*for generations*' (I, 100). *The Swan* appears to have played a central role in the history of the village with the names of several publicans mentioned. Samuel Naish in about 1820 *'took the Swan at East Harnham, & improved the front very much, by putting in those Bow windows … he lived there about 3 or 4 years and removed to the Rose & Crown & died there in May 1833'* (I, 42-3). Even before this, the anti Methodist *'Old Beach'* was the publican but *'failed'* at the Swan (I, 50). George Bowns senior, friend of the Smalls, *'kept the Swan Inn … from 1827 until his death in 1850'*. He must have witnessed several tragic events, not only the body retrieved from the river which was brought to his inn, but also a horse hair weaver, named Stone, who lost his life falling from the old fire engine travelling to Britford to extinguish blazing hay ricks. *'The ricks were all consumed, but his body was taken to the Swan Inn, at Harnham'* (I, 104-5). The pub continued to be run by the same family until June 1877 when 35 year old grandson George Bowns *'accidentally drowned by falling headlong into a Cask of Beer, by over reaching himself, and was not found for 2 or 3 Hours'* (II, 49).

Conclusion

Towards the end of his life William Small became morose and introspective, finding it difficult both to pay his rent and his brother John's wages (eg II, 355). But his links with East Harnham remained strong and many of his best observed comments relate to his youth and time spent with his father working on the bridge. The memoirs do indeed provide a first-hand account of life in the village nearly 200 years ago. They are a rich source that has great value for the historian and interested reader alike.

Bibliography

Howells, J and Newman, R, 2011, *William Small's Cherished Memories and Associations*, WRS, volume 64
RCHM(E), 1980, *Ancient and historical monuments in the city of Salisbury* Vol1, HMSO

Notes

1   WSA 2713/2. These two handwritten volumes of William Small's *Cherished Memories and Associations* were acquired by the Wiltshire and Swindon History Centre in 2003. They appear to have been written between January and September 1881, completed in William's neat and generally very legible handwriting. The author died in 1890 in

Trinity Hospital, a Salisbury almshouse. The 736 pages have since been transcribed and edited by Jane Howells and Ruth Newman, and published by the Wiltshire Record Society, Volume 64, 2011. Punctuation and spelling are as in the original text. Page references in this article are to the originals, eg I, 48-50 [volume 1, pages 48-50], and can be identified as such in the WRS volume.

2   Battle of Talevera, 27 - 28 July 1809, Peninsular War, England and Spain against France.

3   gillyflower - 'popular name for stock, wallflower, &c., so called from its clove-like smell', Chambers' Etymological Dictionary, 1888. The term could also be applied to carnations or dianthus.

4   An important characteristic of the area between Harnham and Britford as well as elsewhere around Salisbury, was the system of floated water meadows that provided irrigation for an early crop of grass for grazing. William Small was acquainted with the skilled workmen - drowners - employed to maintain the channels and banks. [Cook, H & Williamson, T (eds), 2006, *Water Meadows: History, Ecology and Conservation*, Windgather Press].

5   Mountebanks: hawkers of quack medicines who attracted customers with stories, jokes or tricks. 'Snapping at treacle loaves': similar to apple bobbing, slices of bread were dipped in treacle, smothered in flour, suspended from a bar, and had to be eaten without using the hands.

6   *'tin pots, kettles'* etc: William Small's description is similar to a 'skimmington' or rough music, a noisy procession often aimed at ridiculing an unfaithful husband or wife.

7   WRS 40 1985 *Wiltshire Dissenters; Meeting House Certificates and Registrations 1689 - 1852*. Chandler, J, item 509 meeting house in East Harnham, 1798, mentions Richard Wooff and James Maine.

8   The Cliff, purchased by the War Department in 1928, became known as 'Government House'. It was the official residence of GOC Southern Command. It was demolished in 1972 (RCHME 1980, 170).

9   Harnham House was demolished in 1970 (RCHME 1980, 170).

10 RCHME 1980, 170

Detail from triptych of Virgin and Child. St George's church West
Harnham. Eleanor Warre. (photograph Laura Shapland)

8 The Misses Warre of Parsonage Farm

William Alexander

One of the treasures of St George's church, West Harnham, but not on public view, is an exquisite piece of church art in the form of a small altar triptych. The central panel measures about 19cm (7½ins) across and it shows the head and shoulders of the Virgin Mary in profile holding before her the Christ Child, his face towards hers. The figures are moulded in gesso, a material based on plaster of Paris, pure white, with a background of gently shimmering mother-of-pearl. The simplicity, symmetry, serenity and humanity of this depiction of the Virgin Mother and Child can be very moving, encapsulating as it does the love of the mother for her child and the child for its mother.

Since it is Eleanor Warre's work, it also exhibits consummate artistic skill and craftsmanship, her ability with different materials, her scholarship and her religious faith. The words on the doors of the triptych flanking the central figures are in Greek, translating as 'And the Word was made flesh', taken from the opening passage of St John's gospel, 'In the beginning was the Word … '. An almost identical version of the central panel, but in colour, hangs on view in the Trinity Chapel off the south side of the nave.

The entry for the Warre family in the 1937 edition of *Burke's Landed Gentry* traces their descent from the middle ages, but it will suffice to start with the four sisters' grandparents. Henry Warre of Bindon House, Langford Budville in Somerset, a village west of Taunton, married Mary Calvert in 1832. Henry died in 1876 and by the time of the 1891 census[1] his widow had moved to live with their elder son, the Rev Francis Warre and his wife, in Bemerton between Salisbury and Wilton. She is buried beside her son and daughter-in-law in St John's churchyard. The inscription on her tomb reads 'To the memory of Mary Caroline Felicia Warre wife of Henry Warre Esq of Bindon House in the County of Somerset who died May 27th 1895 aged 87 years.'

They were evidently a wealthy family, the wealth being derived from the port wine shipping trade into and out of Bristol. As an indication of their wealth and status locally, in 1866 a north aisle was added to the parish church of St Peter's, Langford Budville, to accommodate the household of Bindon House. The house is now a hotel 'nestled amongst seven acres of stunning formal and woodland gardens.'[2]

Henry and Mary, grandparents of our Warre sisters, had two sons, the elder being Francis, born in 1834. Francis's younger brother, Edmond, had a distinguished teaching career, becoming Provost of Eton and earning a substantial entry in *The Dictionary of National Biography*. Edmond Warre had several offspring, cousins of the Warre sisters, so it is possible that the descendants of some of them could add to the scanty details we have of the sisters, if they could be traced. Strenuous efforts to do so have so far had little success, the few with whom contact has been made proving unable to add much, if anything, to what is already known about their antecedents.

Francis Warre, the elder brother, went into the church and in 1860 married Ellin Jane Peach, herself a clergy daughter. In 1864 he became vicar of Bere Regis in Dorset, and from there in 1870 vicar of Melksham, until 1890 when he became rector of Bemerton where he remained until his death in 1917, a tenure of 27 years. The church of St John's, Bemerton, was built in the 1850s by the same Thomas Wyatt who designed Wilton parish church, All Saints, Harnham, and other churches in and around Salisbury. Canon Warre and his wife, his mother and one of the four daughters are buried in the corner between the chancel and the south transept. The mother's gravestone is a substantial tomb of the horizontal 'pitched roof' type; the other three, small and simple rectangular stones and crosses laid flat in the turf. A wall-mounted memorial to Francis Warre is in the much smaller medieval church of St Andrew, close to the Rectory, and his portrait hangs in Church House in Crane Street.

None of the four daughters married, and they seem to have

lived mostly with their parents, eventually at the Bemerton Rectory, until their father died in 1917, their mother Ellin having pre-deceased him in 1914. This was of course the poet priest George Herbert's rectory back in the 17th century, much altered and enlarged since his day. The little church of St Andrew is only a few steps away on the opposite side of the road.

At least two, possibly three, of the daughters were born before Francis Warre became vicar of Bere Regis: Sybil Mary 1861, Eleanor ('Nellie') Caroline Felicia 1862, Agnes Margaret 1864, Florence Pauline ('Pol' or 'Polly') 1867.

So far very few works of art have come to light that Nellie Warre made before the family moved to Bemerton. My Alexander grandfather was vicar of Edington, a few miles north of Westbury, from 1911-21. While there he wrote a booklet guide to Edington Priory Church.[3] In it he recounts how, during the time that Francis Warre was vicar of Melksham (1870-90) he was called upon to assist the ailing vicar of Edington in organising the restoration of the Priory Church which began in 1887. In the course of the restoration a new screen was erected under the western arch of the central tower, behind the nave altar. The panels on the screen were painted with figures from the history of the Priory Church by none other than Eleanor Warre, then aged about 25. By the late 1930s this screen was considered inappropriate in an otherwise 14th century building where there was already a fine medieval screen at the entry to the chancel, and it was removed. Through enquiries at Edington and through the internet it has now been traced to Christ Church, Blakenall Heath in Staffordshire, to whom it was apparently given by their vicar in 1940. Both screen and paintings look very fine, to judge from the church website on which, for a time, it was proudly displayed.[4] While the Edington restoration was in progress, Nellie Warre made several finely delineated pencil drawings of the Priory which are now in the Wiltshire Heritage Museum, Devizes.[5] One of these shows the builders' planks laid for trundling their barrows through the south porch.

When in 1890 the family arrived in Bemerton the sisters were all in their twenties. Here they ran classes in art, craftwork and music at the Rectory and taught in the Sunday School. Agnes was the most musically talented of the four. This is from her obituary in the *Salisbury Journal*: 'Miss Warre was a talented musician, and imparted her knowledge and enthusiasm to others by training Church choirs – first at St Michael's, Melksham … and afterwards at Bemerton, and she was organist at both churches. In her earlier days, too, Miss Warre was an amateur artist of considerable ability, and produced many charming pictures, including nature scenes and sketches of children'.[6]

One of the sisters, Pauline or Eleanor – accounts differ – was said to be consumptive. For her benefit the family spent winters in Austria or Switzerland, and until very recently it was supposed that it was there Eleanor learnt her various skills in painting, embroidery, sculpting in gesso, and so forth. Research undertaken by Dr Lynne Walker of the University of London Institute of Historical Research has now revealed that Agnes and Eleanor attended the Melksham School of Art in the early 1880s. In 1883 Eleanor was the outstanding student of the year in the Government examinations conducted by the Science & Art Department at South Kensington, the only student to be awarded two marks of 'excellent'.[7]

Eleanor was responsible for the striking reredos in St John's church, Bemerton, with medlar trees in mosaic below to either side of the altar, (George Herbert had planted a medlar tree at the Rectory). The reredos was intended as a memorial to her parents, so may well have been installed after the sisters moved to West Harnham in 1917. The Petition for a Faculty[8] includes Eleanor's handwritten account and her sketches for the design. The reredos is supposed to represent, as she says, 'the risen Christ as seen by St John at Patmos (Revelations Chapter 1)' and 'to pourtray [sic] the whole of the Creed as it bears upon the life, death, and Resurrection of our Lord, all leading up to that belief in the Holy Trinity which the Incarnation has taught us.' She goes on to describe how each element of the design illustrates those concepts. Nikolaus Pevsner says of it: 'Reredos, and handsome mosaic and gesso frieze below of medlar trees. This is probably of the time of Ponting's restoration, ie of 1896.' He was wrong about the date, but the word 'handsome' is noteworthy. Pevsner is sparing with compliments.[9]

Along the base of the reredos are four moulded golden medallions representing the Four Winged Creatures around the throne in St John's vision: the Winged Man or Angel, the Lion, the Bull and the Eagle, adopted later as emblems of the four gospel writers, quite difficult to discern from a distance but worth close examination.

Past inventories [10] for both St John's and St Andrew's indicate that she produced other furnishings for the churches, including three altar frontals and two altar vases, but it seems none of these has survived. An undated design[11] for riddel posts and curtains for the altar at St Peter's, Fugglestone, are not to be seen there now.

Evidence that Nellie Warre's reputation extended beyond the confines of the parishes in which she lived comes from the St Thomas's church parish magazine of May 1918, with a report to the Vestry Meeting regarding 'the new carpet recently laid in the South Chapel of St Thomas's Church. It would interest the Vestry to know that H M Queen Mary had given permission for a piece of the carpet used in Westminster Abbey at the Coronation [1911] to be lent as a pattern for the carpet supplied [to St Thomas's] by the Wilton Carpet Factory. The carpet, designed by Miss E Warre, contained Roses for England, Lilies for the Blessed Virgin Mary, Choughs for St Thomas, and the Merchants' Marks for the Weavers' Guild, William Swayne and John Webb.'

It would be interesting to see the design of this carpet and to know its dimensions and colours. It was evidently not made by the Wilton factory for the coronation or they would surely have had the pattern to work from in 1918. The factory's surviving records lack any reference to it. It is strange that Nellie Warre herself was unable to supply the pattern, but the sisters had only just moved from Bemerton to the Old Parsonage, so maybe it had yet to emerge from the depths of a packing case. Enquiries at county and national archives, including Westminster Abbey, have so far elicited no further information.

An anecdote, possibly apocryphal,[12] of Nellie Warre's time at Bemerton is worth repeating. Acting upon a dream, her father being absent at the time, she dug a hole in the floor of St Andrew's, the little George Herbert church, close to the altar. There, sure enough, she discovered some bones, which she declared to be those of George Herbert whose burial place was hitherto unknown. Her father, upon his return, was exceedingly displeased. Nevertheless, despite the lack of corroborating evidence, there is now a small plaque to George Herbert on the wall adjacent to the spot. Sadly, as so often happens with local traditions, there exists a less romantic version of the story. Bones were indeed

The Old Parsonage 2012 (photograph Jan Howells)

found beneath the floor of the chancel area of St Andrew's by the diocesan architect C E Ponting during restoration work in the 1890s. However, Eleanor Warre had been left to oversee the work in her father's absence, so it is still possible that it was her dream that prompted Ponting's men to excavate and make the discovery.

There is a small brass plaque in St George's church, West Harnham, to the memory of Mr Purvis of The Old Parsonage, who died in 1917, the year in which Canon Warre also died. The four Warre sisters must needs vacate the Rectory which had been their home for 27 years; so they bought The Old Parsonage, which stands on the junction where Harnham Road, Netherhampton Road and Lower Street meet, recognisable by its timbered west wall. Three of them lived together there. The youngest, Pauline ('Pol' or 'Polly') chose to live separately in the thatched cottage belonging to The Parsonage at the turning into the Town Path. The oldest part of The Parsonage dates from the 16th century, but has been added to at later periods.

In buying The Old Parsonage they had in fact purchased a working farm, with land on both sides of the River Nadder and across the road southwards to the foot of Harnham Hill. All the houses in Lower Street down to the Town Path belonged to it and were occupied by farm and household employees. The farm dairyman's daughter, Gwen Trevallion (née Parsons), born in one these cottages lived her whole life there and died only two years ago. Sadly, in her later years she was reluctant to talk about her life there and what she remembered of the Warre sisters, though she did from time to time let fall nuggets of information.

Agnes Warre ran the farm, with such energy and authority that, according to Gwen, she was nicknamed 'The General'. Where children were concerned her preference was for boys. When she called at the cottage where Gwen and her family lived, she sometimes brought gifts for the boys, but never for Gwen. Gwen's experience is borne out by Agnes's obituary: 'Another aspect of Miss Warre's character was her great affection for boys. At the beginning of the century she took a house in Wimborne, and made a home for a series of boys - three or four at a time - attending Queen Elizabeth Grammar School. Many of the boys remained friends for life, and she received letters from them, now grown men, and numbering among them an admiral, from all over the world.'[13]

Agnes was the most active of the four in parish affairs. She was instrumental in providing the land on which the Harnham Scout Hut was built and in the formation of the troop, and was one of the original members of the West Harnham Parochial Church Council, formed in 1920 following the Act of Parliament passed to give the laity a greater say in running parishes. She sat on the board of management that in 1920 purchased, erected and ran the Harnham Parish Hall (now Harnham Memorial Hall), as a memorial to those who fell in the First World War.[14] She also took a keen interest in the church choir, and did the congregation a dubious favour by donating a Hammond electric organ to replace the harmonium.

In The Parsonage the sisters had two maids and a cook, all of whom wore uniforms, different for morning and afternoon. The younger maid wore a frilly cap. Miss Margaret Smith, who supplied this information, was regularly sent to buy eggs from the farm, and remembers three elderly ladies in long dresses walking in single file from The Parsonage to the church, where they sat in separate pews. One was by then very deaf, and a special device had been installed in the Trinity Chapel to assist her hearing. Since two of the sisters had died by the time Miss Smith is recalling, her recollection of three was a mystery until it transpired that in their later years they were joined by a companion, Miss A M Eckett, who is buried close to them at St George's with an identical grave stone.

So far, despite exhaustive enquiries, only two photographs of any of the sisters have been found. One shows two of them in their pony and trap in front of The Parsonage in the 1920s. Agnes is wearing a round-topped hat with a band. The other occupant is almost certainly Eleanor, since Sybil had died in 1919 and Pauline tended to keep apart from the others. The white boundary stone against the wall reads '1904 City of Salisbury'. East Harnham had become part of the city in that year. In 1927 West Harnham followed suit, so the stone would have been replaced with one a

mile or so further to the west. The young man holding the pony has been identified as Reginald Davis, whose son still lives in Harnham. The second photograph is of Agnes (note the same hat!) with a favourite cow, in the field next to the river which is now used for cricket and general recreation.

Like the Rectory from which they had moved, The Parsonage was little more than a stone's throw from the parish church of St George. Actually one half of a parish church, since the parish of East and West Harnham had been created in 1881 with two churches, All Saints in the east and St George's in the west. In its dimensions, age and character, St George's is altogether different from St John's, Bemerton. The building dates from the 12th century and has obvious Norman features. It is small, plain, intimate and inconspicuous. So inconspicuous that the chapter on churches in the Salisbury volume of the *Victoria County History* ignores it altogether, and until recently many Salisbury residents were unaware of its existence. As may be imagined, the four sisters immersed themselves in the life and work of the church, and Eleanor in particular set about alleviating its plainness, working in her studio at the bottom of the garden, which can still be seen.

Quite soon after the sisters arrived in Harnham, a sad event occurred which gave Eleanor a good reason for applying her artistic talents to the embellishment of St George's, when the eldest sister, Sybil Mary died in 1919. At the time there was no stained glass in the church, so Eleanor created a design for the east window above the main altar. In the two principal lights are angels robed as Israelite priests, as described in Leviticus Chapter 8. These were to be attendants upon the figure of the Eternal Priest, modelled in gesso and partly gilded, which was to stand against the central mullion; which it did until fairly recently when permission was obtained to move it into the aperture between the nave and the Trinity Chapel. The quatrefoil light at the top of the window shows a triangular representation of the Holy Trinity: Pater (Father), Filius (Son) and Spiritus (Holy Spirit) at the three corners, all linked to Deus (God) in the centre. The inscription reads 'Alleluia, Alleluia, To the Glory of God in memory of Sybil Mary Warre.' The draft design to accompany the Petition for a Faculty is in the Wiltshire and Swindon History Centre.[15] The varied colours of the angels' robes and the subtle shades of blue in the background, together with the carefully designed pattern

East window, St George's church West Harnham. Eleanor Warre. (photograph Laura Shapland)

of the lead tracery make for an effective composition. This and the Trinity Chapel window were installed by the London firm of Powell, which was also responsible for much glass in Salisbury Cathedral and elsewhere.

The two lancet south windows of the chancel[16] also contain stained glass to Eleanor's designs. At the top of each of these is an angel playing a medieval musical instrument, horn and harp. Below are scenes of Jesus preaching. The background imitates the strapwork pattern found in some Salisbury Cathedral windows.

Another opportunity for a memorial window came with the death in 1925 of the Rev Geoffry Hill, who had served the parish as vicar for 34 years, and who merits a brief digression. Much beloved by his parishioners, a bachelor assisted in his parish work by his sister Mrs Grimes, he was a great promoter of parish activities, especially the church choirs. In 1906 he founded the Harnham Fife and Bugle Band, membership of which was conditional on joining the church choir. He founded the Harnham cricket club and captained the team until well into his sixties. In one of his last matches a rising ball struck him on the cheek breaking his dentures. His only anxiety was about his services and sermons, the following day being Sunday. By an extraordinary piece of good fortune, two members of the team were dental mechanics, and they worked most of the night to provide him with new ones in time for the next day's services. He was also no mean scholar. Among his publications is one entitled *The Aspirate: the use of the letter H in English, Latin, Greek and Gaelic*. Of more interest locally is his *Wiltshire Folk Songs and Carols*, some of which he collected from old folk in Britford.[17]

All in all, a vicar worthy of a memorial, which Nellie Warre duly provided in the east window of the Trinity Chapel off the south side of the nave, appropriately symbolic of the Holy Trinity. For God the Father there are four medallions, as on the Bemerton St John's reredos, representing the Four Living Creatures of the Book of Revelation, and the banner legend 'I am that I am', God's response when Moses asked what the Israelites were to call God. God the Son is shown by the Crucifixion flanked by the Virgin Mary and St John. Above them hovers the Holy Spirit in the form of a dove surrounded by the Seven Flames. Higher still, two more angel musicians are playing a lyre and a tambourine. The foliage background in the upper part of the window is clearly 'arts and crafts' inspired. The inscription reads 'To the glory of God and in memory of the Rev Geoffry Hill, vicar of East and West Harnham 1891-1925'. The window cost £88 and was dedicated in 1930.[18]

In 1939, three years after Nellie Warre had died, stained glass panels were inserted in the two pairs of lancet windows in the south wall of the Trinity Chapel by the firm of A J Dix, almost certainly from drawings left by Eleanor.[19] Four more angels are playing an aulos (a curious double trumpet), a psaltery (an early plucked instrument), a rebec or viol, and cymbals. It has been noticed recently that these instruments, eight in all, are the same as those being played by the carved angels at the ends of the choir stalls in Salisbury Cathedral, so it is likely that they served as her models.

Also made to Nellie's designs, and under the supervision of herself and her sisters, were two fine altar frontals. They recruited and trained a working party of local women for the purpose.[20] The red frontal for Palm Sunday, Pentecost and saints' days was renovated in 2012 but is no longer complete, mice having eaten five of the six tassels that once adorned the bottom edge. The white one for Christmas, Easter and other major festivals is very finely embroidered with floral designs and gold braid, on shimmering white silk which is now too fragile for the frontal to be used.

Included in the 1922 Faculty for the main east window were two movable altar triptychs, designed and made by Eleanor Warre, one for Easter, the other for Christmas. The Christmas triptych and the small triptych of Mother and Child already described were opened on Christmas Eve 1922, as recounted in the *Parish Magazine*: 'The fourth Sunday in Advent being also Christmas Eve, when the last hymn, A.M.58 was given out, the doors of the Christmas Triptych were opened, and the pictures of the Nativity displayed to view; also on the small alter [sic] a little low relief of the Mother and Babe, with the Greek text, 'The Word Became Flesh'.' Hymn 58 in the old Ancient & Modern hymnbook describes the visit of the shepherds to the manger. The fourth verse runs 'But, oh, what sight appears/ Within that lowly door!/ A manger, stall and swaddling clothes,/ A child, a Mother poor!' A perfect cue for opening the triptych doors to reveal the manger scene. The paintings are on stiff paper which unfortunately shows signs of deterioration.

The Easter triptych, which shows in its central panel the risen Christ breaking bread with the two disciples who met him on the road to Emmaus, formed with the main east window part of the memorial to Sybil Warre. The gesso figures in the side panels are of two virgin martyrs, St Ursula and St Agnes. The central panel, painted in egg tempera over a gesso base, has suffered from woodworm. So far, none of the experts consulted have been able to recommend conservation treatment that might not damage the painting itself.

The central panel of the third seasonal triptych is of the Presentation of the infant Christ in the Temple, and is displayed between Christmas and Easter. Anna the Prophetess has the Babe in her arms. The background is mother-of-pearl.

The four sisters died in the same order as they were born, the oldest Sybil in 1919 as we have seen. Eleanor ('Nellie'), died in 1936 and is commemorated in a stained glass panel inserted in the leper squint between the Trinity Chapel and the south porch, which reads: 'The triptych [sic; there were 4], the painted

Detail from Christmas triptych, St George's Church West Harnham. Eleanor Warre. (Photograph Laura Lapland)

windows [sic; they were stained glass] of the Chancel & the Trinity Chapel, were designed by Eleanor Caroline Felicia Warre.' An obituary appeared in the *Salisbury Times* for Friday 30 October 1936: 'The death occurred at her home on Thursday of last week of Miss Eleanor Caroline Felicia Warre, of Parsonage Farmhouse, Harnham. Miss Warre who had been in failing health for some time, was 74 years of age and was the second daughter of the late Canon Warre, a former rector of Bemerton. She was well-known in Salisbury and the county, and was a highly respected member of St George's Church, West Harnham, in which parish she had lived for some considerable time. Much of her life had been devoted to painting, and several examples of her works are still to be seen in the church, a notable example being the east window. She was also responsible for the three triptychs portraying the seasons of the year, and for the hangings and other fabric … Another memory of her is the omnibus shelter which has been erected in West Harnham [beside The Parsonage, recently rebuilt], which she gave to the parish.'

It goes on to describe her funeral which was taken by the Bishop of Sherborne, and concludes: 'The floral tributes included wreaths from the employees of the farm, the organist and choir of St George's Church, the Bishop of Sherborne and Mrs Allen and the Harnham Boys' Football Club.'

Agnes, who ran the farm, died in 1946. Obituaries, quoted earlier, appeared in both local newspapers. Pauline, the youngest, died in 1948.[21]

After Pauline died, a complicated will[22] had to be sorted out, one of the eventual outcomes being a bequest of £40,000 to St George's Church, in trust, the income to be used to pay a curate's stipend. If there is no stipendiary curate the interest may be used for other purposes. The PCC were able to buy at a favourable price the land on which the Church Hall now stands, and the Scout Troop likewise the other part of the field. Much of the rest of the farmland was given to the parish and the city. That includes the recreation ground beside the river Nadder and Parsonage Green on the south side of Netherhampton Road. Their name is perpetuated in the Warre Allotments below Harnham Hill. Pauline herself left about £3,000 to Bemerton parish to be used to repair the church and augment the income of the incumbent.

Three of the sisters are buried in St George's churchyard in the corner formed by the south wall of the chancel and the east wall of the Trinity Chapel. As with their parents at Bemerton, the graves are marked by small square stones and separate crosses laid flat in the turf. Pauline elected to be buried close to her parents and grandmother at St John's, Bemerton.

It would be invidious for one untutored in art and aesthetics to pass judgement on the quality of Eleanor Warre's artistic work. However, an authoritative assessment is provided by Dr Lynne Walker, who visited to see Eleanor's artwork in 2005 and wrote to the Vicar thus:

> Eleanor was a skilful draftsperson as her work in your church and at Bemerton and the drawings in Wiltshire Record Office confirm. She is typical of women designers of this period who under the influence of the Gothic Revival and the Arts and Crafts Movement of Morris and Ruskin designed and made church art in diverse media: stained glass, mosaic, gesso, embroidery design and painting. With the exception of mosaics all these are present in West Harnham. They are valuable, and need to be treasured individually for their quality and beauty, but as a group they are especially important as representative of the best work produced by women amateur designers of church art in Britain. Moreover, as part of social history, Eleanor Warre and her sisters were typical of many women of the period whose fathers were vicars in the Church of England and whose art, and belief, were facilitated by their parents' occupation and position in the church.[23]

Acknowledgements

Clare Eagle, for photographs; Robert Eberhard, for information regarding stained glass window makers; Sue Johnson, for information regarding the Coronation carpet and Edington Priory drawings; Robert Salkeld, for his efforts to track down Warre relatives, drawings and photographs; Eileen Saunders, for the recollections of two friends who attended The Warre sisters' classes in Bemerton; Canon David Scrace, for permission to use photographs of EW's artwork in St George's church; Margaret Smith, for childhood reminiscences of the sisters at The Parsonage; Gwen Trevallion (now deceased), whose father was farm dairyman; Anne Trevett, for information regarding the Warre sisters in Bemerton, including the discovery of George Herbert's bones.

Bibliography

Alexander, Ernest Christian, 1921, *Edington Church Wiltshire: Notes on Church and Monastery,* Massey & Co

Harnham Women's Institute, *Scrapbook of Harnham,* 1954-6, (Rev Geoffry Hill photo & anecdotes.)

Matthew, HGC & Harrison, Brian (eds), 2004, *The Oxford Dictionary of National Biography.* Oxford University Press.

Pevsner, Nikolaus, 1963, (Rev ed 1975), *The Buildings of England: Wiltshire,* Penguin.

Pirie-Gordon, H (ed), 1937, *Burke's Landed Gentry,* Shaw Publishing.

St Thomas's Church, Salisbury. *Parish Magazine,* May 1918. Report of Vestry Meeting. (EW's carpet for the 1911 Coronation.)

East & West Harnham Parish Magazine , Feb 1923. Opening of the Christmas Triptych.

STM, 30 Oct 1936, p 9 obituary of Miss Eleanor Caroline Felicia Warre

SJL, 24 May 1946, p 7 obituary of Miss Agnes Mary Warre

Notes

1   1891 Census, RG12/1622, folio 4

2   Small, Julia, *Henry Warre,* in *Notes on the history of the Bindon estate in Langford Budvillle and Milverton, Somerset: compiled 1981-84,* p 44 -50. Unpublished typescript. SANHS AR6 77, Somerset Heritage Centre. www.warre.com; www.langfordbudville.org./history.html; http://bindon.com

3   Alexander, 1921

4   www.churches.lichfield.anglican.org/walsall/blakenallheath/christc.htm

5   Wiltshire Heritage Museum, Devizes items DZSWS: 1982.8105-7

6   *SJL* 24 May 1946

7   Walker, Lynne, 2012, 'Eleanor Warre and her contemporaries', talk to Bemerton Local History Society. 15 November, 2012. *Devizes & Wilts Gazette,* 29 November 1883, p3

8   WSA D/1/61/54/49 *Faculty, Petition* (29 Oct 1917). Reredos in St John's, Bemerton

9   Pevsner, 1975, p 107

10   WSA D1/5/2/232. *Inventory of Church Goods in the Parish Church of St John Bemerton in the Rural Deanery of Wilton.* nd. 'Reredos: designed and executed by Miss Eleanor Warre and given as a memorial to her parents (1918)'.

     WSA D1/5/3/231. *Inventory of Church Goods in the Parish Church of St Andrew Bemerton in the Rural Deanery of Wilton.* nd. 'Altar cloths and linen: 3 frontals – all designed by Miss E Warre - white one represents the Burning Bush, the red with 4 Evangelists, the blue represents St Andrew's Cross. (These were worked by Diocesan Guild). Other vessels: 2 Altar vases – each hand-beaten out of one piece of copper –

designed by Miss Eleanor Warre.

11   WSA 1874/6 undated design for riddel posts and curtains for the altar at St Peter's, Fugglestone

12   Information from Anne Trevett

13   *SJL* 24 May 1946

14   WSA 776/970 Harnham Parish hall: indenture between Sir James Macklin and Harnham War Memorial Committee 8 May 1920

15   WSA D1/61/62/15 *Faculty, Petition* (31 Jan 1922). St George's Church, main east window

16   WSA D1/61/79/30 *Faculty, Minor* (16 Mar 1934). St George's, stained glass chancel south windows.

17   Harnham Women's Institute Scrapbook of Harnham 1954-6

18   WSA D1/61/72/1 *Faculty, Proclamation* (28 Nov 1929). St George's Trinity Chapel east window

19   WSA D1/61/87/87 *Faculty, Minor* (16 Nov 1938). St George's, stained glass Trinity Chapel south side & leper squint.

20   *Dedication of red altar frontal. 27 January 1925.* Contemporary typed sheet in scrapbook compiled by Harold K Trevallion (d 1991) churchwarden, West Harnham. Harnham Parish Archives. *West Harnham. Anniversary Commemoration of St George's Church.* SJL 25 April 1930 p 8 includes dedication of white altar frontal and oak reredos in Trinity Chapel 'also designed and given by Miss Eleanor Warre'.

21   Pauline Warre death notice *STM* 17 April 1948 p 8

22   *The will dated 10 June 1937 and Five Codicils of Miss Agnes Margaret Warre deceased. Testatrix died 21 May 1946. Proved 19 September 1946.* Jonas & Parker, Salisbury (Solicitors). *Will of Miss Florence Pauline Warre. Died 17 April 1948. Proved 28 July 1948.* Jonas &Parker, Salisbury.

23   Private communication. See also Walker, L, 2011, 'Women and church art' in *Churches 1870-1914,* The Victorian Society Studies in Victorian Architecture and Design, Volume 3

View from Harnham Hill. *Mate's Illustrated Guide*, Salisbury, 1905

9 East Harnham joins the city 1871–1911

Helen Wilcockson

At the turn of the 19th century, Salisbury's population was growing rapidly and the city needed more land on which to house its citizens. On the southern side of the River Avon, at the only crossing point giving, access to the city from the south, was East Harnham, a village with plenty of space, where developers were beginning to build new houses.[1]

In March 1904 a Local Government Inquiry was held in Salisbury, after which the boundaries were changed, resulting in East Harnham being absorbed into the city. The consequence was that East Harnham was supplied with pure drinking water, and had its sewage safely drained away. This, plus the availability of excellent building land, transformed the village into a prosperous and popular suburb of Salisbury.

Study of the Census Enumerators Books (CEBs) have shown that from 1871[2] East Harnham was a village in decline, with the majority of the male population involved in some form of agricultural employment. The 1901 CEB[3] shows that while some were still employed as agricultural labourers, there were now many professional people and businessmen living in East Harnham. In the decade before 1901 there had been a slight increase in the population, (just 21 people) as several new houses had been constructed since the previous census.

The principal primary source for this paper is the evidence given to the Borough Extension Inquiry (BEI), which was held between 2-4 March 1904, plus all its supporting documents. The

Inquiry had been advertised throughout the city, and the report is a printed verbatim account of every word uttered, and by whom, during the consultations.

A list of counsel and solicitors representing the various interested bodies, and landowners appears on the first page. Every witness had to submit in advance a written 'proof of evidence', containing a statement of their occupation and opinions regarding the need to extend Salisbury's boundaries. This applied to East Harnham, and to the other two areas under discussion, namely Fisherton Anger Without, and Milford Without. It has thus been possible to cross check the written evidence, against what was actually said at the Inquiry.

Reading the 'Memorial'[4] attached to the front of the report, it is obvious that the Salisbury City Council was not only worried about the possible health hazards due to there being no proper drainage in the three areas it was proposing to absorb, but also that new houses were being built without any system of supervision, or adherence to proper building standards.

It was reported that the 'County Medical Officer of Health (MOH) knows of no other town in England where the inhabitants are congested in so small an area'.[5] These sentiments were corroborated by the Medical Officers of Health for Salisbury and Liverpool.[6]

In1904 the city of Salisbury covered 600 acres, and evidence showed that Salisbury's population density was 30 people to the acre. If the area and population of the Cathedral Close were removed then the density rose to 45.[7] In 1901 East Harnham had a resident population (excluding the Alderbury Union Workhouse) of 315 on 371 acres, a density of 1.1.[8]

To compound the problem, following the passing of the Military Lands Act in 1872, the British Army required a new training area, and Salisbury Plain was recognised as being suitable.[9] 'The Head Quarters of the Second Army Corps having been recently established in Salisbury', there was increased pressure for accommodation in which to house its personnel.[10]

The East Harnham evidence provided to the Inquiry, is supported by the Parish Council Minute Book.[11] Unlike the Borough Extension Inquiry this is simply a record of decisions made at each meeting, there is no account of discussion, agreements or disagreements. However it is an authentic primary source, with

M Hall – Gaskill, W,
·06. *Wiltshire Leaders,*
cial & Political,
ueenhithe, between
240 and 241

every Minute signed by the Chairman Mr Robert Hall, a local
solicitor.

Several members of the East Harnham Parish Council, including Mr R Hall, and Mr A C Botham, were witnesses to the Inquiry. It was stated that everyone living in East Harnham wished
to be taken into Salisbury.[12] When Winchester, another cathedral
city extended its boundaries in 1900, it had to cope with the,
'utmost hostility' from its citizens.[13]

The only dissenting voice was Lord Radnor, the major landowner. But in many ways the Radnors were responsible for the

start of new house building in East Harnham. In August 1894, 150 acres of their land above the village was sold, having been widely advertised in the *Salisbury & Winchester Journal*.[14] The advertisement stressed the picturesque nature of the site, and the quantity and quality of the land for sale. A year later there was a sale of a further 66 acres, to the west of Coombe Road. The auctioneer's catalogue for this sale identified the size and location of every plot, extolling the healthy virtues of the site.[15]

The land was bought by Mr James Lyewood a property developer, who began to build substantial houses. He had to sink a well on the top of Harnham Hill,[16] and provided drainage into cesspools above East Harnham. At the Inquiry it was pointed out that in the 'opinion of the County Medical Officer of Health, that polluting matter will travel great distances through fissures in the chalk'.[17]

Comparing the 1881 Ordnance Survey map, with the one for 1901 shows that considerable development had occurred in East Harnham several years before the Inquiry, and other evidence supports this. In the 1870s building byelaws had come into operation nationally, controlling the size of houses, and the space between them.

Mr Robert Hall, Chairman of the East Harnham Parish Council stated 'that no building byelaws have been adopted',[18] implying that if the village came within the city then there would be greater control over property development. He told the Inquiry that he lived in one of the newly built houses, and that the cesspools drained into the River Avon. He also added that there were two new estates under construction, and that there would soon be more.[19]

It was pointed out again and again that all the building land within the city of Salisbury had been used up; all that was left was the Cathedral Close, the Greencroft, and the water meadows, which were unsuitable. Alderman George Fulford, a former mayor, presented an excellent witness statement on the state of housing in Salisbury.[20] In it he declared that many of the old courts and alleys had been pulled down to make way for better housing. He pointed out that the land in the Friary, at Wyndham Park and the site of the old County Gaol had been built on, and that there was nothing left, within the present borough, that was not covered in streets and houses.

It is (and was) widely acknowledged that there is a close connection between 'bad housing and bad health, and public opinion was shocked to think that by permitting insanitary conditions it was not saving money but losing it,'[21] and Briggs passed a similar comment, 'it costs more to create disease than prevent it'.[22] Evidence given to the Inquiry demonstrated that these statements were correct when applied to Salisbury and East Harnham.

In answer to questioning, Mr A C Botham the City Surveyor said that during the previous ten years, 627 houses had been built in Salisbury (Wyndham Park and the Friary), and between 1894 and 1904, 39 houses had been built in East Harnham, the majority of them being substantial properties.[23] Many people who

A C Bothams
Dorling, EE, 1906,
Wiltshire and Dorset
the Opening of the
Twentieth Century,
Contemporary
Biographies, Pike & Co,
162

had previously lived in Salisbury, including solicitors, and retired service personnel, had moved out there.

Towards the end of the 19th century Salisbury was becoming a much more prosperous city, especially since the arrival of the railway in the middle of the century. The City Surveyor informed the Inquiry that there had been a considerable loss of building land to the railway, and also for the necessity of providing better roads to meet the increased traffic.[24]

While all this new building work was going on in East Harnham, the people living in the 'old part' of the village, down near the river, had to cope with terrible sanitary conditions. Many of the witnesses described in great detail the foul circumstances that existed for their water supply and the removal of nuisances. Written and spoken evidence to the Inquiry, together with the Parish Council Minutes, reveal that the villagers had to contend with badly contaminated drinking water. Random testing commissioned by the Parish Council showed that three out of the five drinking water wells were heavily polluted, the most badly affected was at the Rose and Crown.[25]

This was caused by the old privy vaults being in close proximity to the wells 'which are shallow in nature',[26] and the cesspools from the higher ground above the village also drained into these wells. The Alderbury Union Workhouse had been built above the village, and it too had a contaminated well. After East Harnham was absorbed into Salisbury, the water supply would be pure, coming from deep wells sunk into the chalk north of the city.

It could be argued that the evidence given by the East Harnham residents was biased, and exaggerated the poor conditions in order to gain better facilities. That this was not so, was demonstrated by the testimonies of independent evidence to the Inquiry.

A key witness was Dr Hope, MOH for Liverpool. In his report on the conditions in East Harnham he noted that 'both soakage and surface washings into the wells is unavoidable',[27] and 'the tenants informed me that they had repeatedly complained without effect'. Several entries in the Parish Council Minute Book support these remarks, recording occasions when neglectful or irresponsible landlords had been called to a meeting for the complaints to be registered.[28] Dr Hope commented that he was not 'aware of the existence in any city of conditions so filthy, and so insanitary as I have seen in some of the cottage properties'. At the same time he was impressed by the 'cleanly and respectable condition of the inhabitants',[29] demonstrating that the villagers did their best to try and live decently in spite of the filth and contamination.

The MOH for Salisbury, Dr Harcourt Coates said 'without doubt the city has outgrown its capabilities for housing, not only for the better classes but what is in my opinion, far more important the artisan and labouring classes'. He went on to say that he hesitated to condemn many of the cottages 'because of the absolute impossibility of finding dwellings into which the work-

THE PUBLIC HEALTH ACT, 1875.

NEW SARUM (SALISBURY)

WHEREAS the Town Council of the City of New Sarum have applied to the Local Government Board for sanction to borrow money for purposes of Sewerage and Sewage Disposal, including the construction of works in the Parishes of East Harnham, Fisherton Anger Without, Stratford under the Castle, Milford Without, Britford, and West Harnham, in the Rural District of Salisbury; and the Local Government Board have directed Inquiry into the subject-matter of such Application:

NOTICE IS HEREBY GIVEN that Major C. E. Norton, R.E., the Inspector appointed to hold the said Inquiry, will attend for that purpose at the Council House, Salisbury, on Wednesday, the Second day of March, 1904, at Ten o'clock in the Forenoon, and will then and there be prepared to receive the evidence of any persons interested in the matter of the said Inquiry.

S. B. PROVIS,
Secretary.

Local Government Board,
12th February, 1904.

Printed by Waterlow Bros. & Layton, Limited, 24 and 25, Birchin Lane, London, E.C.   13238—450—2-4

Poster. Improvements necessary following boundary extension. 1904. WSA 410/14

ing classes could move'.[30] Demand for better quality housing for working people grew. The passing of the Housing of the Working classes Act in 1890, 'provided for the clearance of unhealthy areas'.[31] Evidence taken at the Inquiry suggested that Salisbury had rather dragged its feet. Assistance became available as engineering and medical technology improved. Eventually new terraced houses were built in the other two 'added areas' to meet this need, and some land was made available for the erection of smaller houses in East Harnham.

In East Harnham houses were built on two housing estates for the middle and upper classes, wanting to live in pleasanter surroundings overlooking the city. Those who could afford it moved into these properties, although the developer complained that he was having problems selling land because of the lack of proper drainage.[32]

One of the main reasons for East Harnham's enthusiasm for the boundary extension was that it stood to gain financially. Salisbury agreed to provide a good clean water supply, and the sewage would be pumped over Harnham Bridge and into the main city sewer, to be drained away into the newly enlarged and improved treatment plant at Bugmore. The cost to do this work for East Harnham was £6,192, of which the village had to contribute £1,507.[33] Naturally all this expenditure must have incurred a rate rise, by how much is not known. Salisbury had to borrow money in order to improve the infrastructure of the city.

It is interesting to note that there had been discussion, confirmed by examination of the relevant Parish Council Minute Books, of each of the 'added areas' embarking on the construction of their own sewage treatment facilities, 'which would have been a bad thing for Salisbury, to have its suburbs spoilt by the establishment of more sewage farms'.[34]

Another bonus of the boundary extension was 'that since the village is now becoming a residential district of Salisbury' the school at East Harnham would come under the control of the Local Education Committee.[35]

'The Local Government Board if satisfied with the sewerage and sewage disposal of the city will sanction the desired extension of the Borough boundaries'.[36] Developments took place quickly, once the Inquiry in March 1904 was over. By August of that year the Local Government Board's Confirmation (No 11) Act

1904 was issued confirming the extension of the city boundaries. This came into operation in November when an enlarged Town Council was elected.

Salisbury, where there was evidence of serious overcrowding, needed more space in order to accommodate its population in better healthier houses. In extending its boundaries, Salisbury gained access to building land on which to house its citizens. Conditions in East Harnham in 1904 were appalling, with the village having neither pure water nor good drainage. Following the Inquiry it obtained both mainly at Salisbury's expense, so allowing it to develop into the pleasant suburb it is today.

Bibliography

Briggs, A, 1963, *Victorian Cities*, Penguin Books

James, N D G, 1987, *Plain Soldering*, Hobnob Press

McAlister, G, & McAlister E, G, 1941, *Town & Country Planning*, Faber & Faber

VCH Wilts 4

VCH Wilts 6

Wilcockson, H, 1998, *Metamorphosis of East Harnham 1871-1911*, unpublished Open University dissertation

WSA at WSHC

G23/133/1 Papers relating to the extension of Borough boundaries and the Local Government Board Inquiry, 1903-6 (hereafter BEI)

G23/951/1 East Harnham Parish Council Minute Book, 1896-1904

776/20 Land sale catalogue 1895

Notes

1 This paper is based on research done as a Final Project Report for Open University Course D301, 1998

2 CEB 1871 RG10 1952, folios 25-32

3 CEB 1901 RG13 1956, folios 13-18

4 BEI Memorial, Item 26 November 1903

5 KC for Salisbury, BEI Day 1, p3

6 Proof of evidence MOH Liverpool, BEI Day 2, p32

7 City Surveyor's evidence, BEI Day 1, p32

8 BEI Memorial, p5

9 James, 14

10 BEI Memorial, Item 19

11 G23/951/1, 18 January 1904

12 ibid

13 Letters from chairmen of parish councils in Winchester to the Local Government Board 11 & 14 October 1899, Hampshire Record Office W/C1/5/570

14 *SJL* June & July 1894
15 WSA 776/20
16 Proof of evidence Mr J Lyewood
17 Salisbury's KC, BEI Day 1, p4
18 Proof of evidence Mr R Hall
19 BEI Day 2, p103
20 Alderman Fulford's witness statement
21 McAlister & McAlister, p31
22 Briggs, p31
23 BEI Statistical Information
24 City Surveyor's evidence
25 WSA G23/951/1, 18 January 1897
26 City Surveyor's evidence, BEI Day 1, p40
27 Dr Hope's proof of evidence
28 WSA G23/951/1, 20 March 1897
29 Dr Hope's proof of evidence
30 Dr Harcourt Coates MOH for Salisbury proof of evidence
31 McAlister & McAlister p38
32 Mr J Lyewood (property developer) proof of evidence
33 Salisbury's KC, Day 3, p121
34 Editorial *SJL*, 5 March 1904
35 Mr G Harris (Clerk of the Local Education Committee) proof of evidence
36 Letter dated 3 March 3 1903 from the Town Clerk to Sir A Binnie (civil engineer for the sewerage scheme)

10 From Pearly Gates to Memorial Hall

William Alexander

A Parish Hall for Harnham

On Wednesday afternoon 22 September 1920, The Rev Geoffry Hill, Vicar of Harnham, presented Mrs Radcliffe with a silver key with which to unlock the door, and the building we now know as Harnham Memorial Hall – then The Parish Hall – was officially opened. Mrs Radcliffe had been chosen for the honour because she had started the subscription list with a gift of £100. No fewer than ten people made speeches and the Harnham Girls Choir sang 'Land of Hope and Glory'. Later that evening a social gathering and entertainment for 130 guests was held in the Hall, with dancing until 2 am!

In May of the previous year, 1919, a public meeting had been held to launch a Harnham War Memorial Fund, and to discuss how best to commemorate those who had died in the Great War. A fourfold scheme was proposed: to place tablets in both churches inscribed with the names of the fallen; to erect a Parish

Harnham Memorial Hall (photograph Laura Shapland)

Hall; to place in the Hall a Roll of Honour board recording the names of all the Harnham men who had served in the forces, with crosses against those who had fallen; and to purchase land for an extension to All Saints churchyard.

Sir James Macklin of West Tytherley offered to sell for £250 land he owned behind the church, for extending the churchyard and building a hall. This offer was accepted, the Memorial Hall Committee paying £50 for the hall plot and the church £200. An elaborate indenture was drawn up legally conveying in trust the land for the erection of a Parish Hall for the Parishes of East and West Harnham.

The Trustees were the Rev Geoffry Hill, Vicar, Alfred Williams, Leonard Ponting, hide and skin merchant, Agnes Warre of The Old Parsonage, and Ernest Russ, schoolmaster. The document records that the £50 purchase price for the land was raised by voluntary subscription. It also stipulates that the hall is to be 'used as a Hall for the promotion of the moral and social welfare of the Parishes of East and West Harnham according and subject to such rules and regulations for the management and governance of the said land and buildings thereon as shall be framed from time to time by the Managing Committee thereof'. The Management Committee was to consist of equal numbers of people from East and West Harnham, elected annually. Among those who witnessed the Trustees' signatures were Grace Jerrim of Saxon Road, schoolmistress, Richard Southcombe of 70 Harnham Road and Lloyds Bank, and Alice Eckett, spinster, of The Old Parsonage.

The Pearly Gates

The Committee had been lucky to acquire so promptly a convenient plot of land, at what one assumes was a favourable price. Fortune of a more unexpected kind was to favour them again in determining just what sort of hall they wanted and at a price the parish could possibly afford. By a happy coincidence St Edmund's Church in Bedwin Street had decided to dispose of their outlying Mission Church in Winchester Street, and in 1920 the Charity Commission gave permission for them to sell it. Sometime after the Harnham public meeting in May 1919 to discuss what form their war memorial should take, the Committee inspected the Mission Church and, having concluded it would

Location of mission church in Winchester Street. OS map 1880 sheet LXVI.11.25

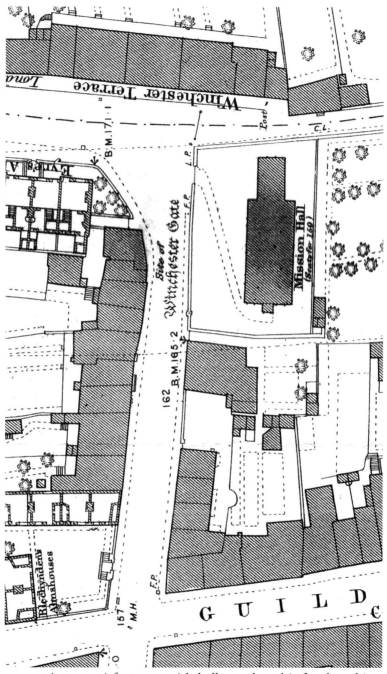

convert into a satisfactory parish hall, purchased it for the asking price of £50.

The building was duly dismantled and re-erected on its present site, with some alterations, in time for the grand opening

Interior of mission
church in Wincheste□
Street, Easter 1920 (?

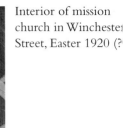

ceremony already described. The cost of removal, reconstruction and furnishing appears to have been about £350, which was raised by means of events and donations. Lady Hulse made an interest free loan of £100.

In 1920 the Mission Church was by no means 'nearly new'. It had begun life in 1866 at the top of Winchester Street at the junction with London Road and Jubilee Terrace, built by Wilkes & Son, ironmongers of 4, Queen Street. The name is on a small cast iron plaque riveted to what is now the north entrance to the Hall. At first it was used as a school for poor inhabitants until, in 1869, a licence was granted to perform divine service there. Kelly's Directory of 1885 describes it as 'St Edmund's (Iron) Mission Church, Winchester St. clergy of St Edmund's; 150 sittings all free; 6.30 pm; weekdays occasional services'. To the residents of the nearby lodging house and Barnards Cross Mission it became known as 'The Pearly Gates'. Eileen O'Leary, who lived at the corner of Guilder Lane and Winchester Street is said to have worshipped there. Tragically, two months after her marriage aged 19 in 1912 she was one of several local people to die in the sinking of the *Titanic*.

To start with the hall was always referred to as The Parish Hall. It is not clear when it began to be called Harnham Memorial Hall, but the change helps to distinguish it from The Church Hall (formerly St George's Hall) built in 1958 at the other end of the parish.

The photograph

A few years ago, in the course of a house clearance in Trinity Street, a large mounted photograph was found which shows what is almost certainly (though it is not named) the interior of the Mission Church decorated for a festival. The numbers on the board are all Easter hymns from an early edition of *Hymns Ancient & Modern*. 'The strife is o'er, the battle done' and 'Christ the Lord is risen today' we still sing, but 'Light's glittering morning bedecks the sky, Heaven thunders forth the victory cry' and 'On the resurrection morning, Soul and body meet again' have been banished from later editions. The photograph is signed S Sutton. Stanley Sutton, photographer, worked from premises in the New Canal from 1919 to 1944. Very possibly this picture was taken at Easter 1920 in the knowledge that the church was about to be closed and dismantled.

The work of taking down and rebuilding the church was carried out by Mr S Clark, with Mr H Messenger acting as architect. Some alterations were made to adapt it for use as a parish hall. The pointed arch above the altar became a horizontal proscenium arch for a stage, and thus the pitch of the roof could

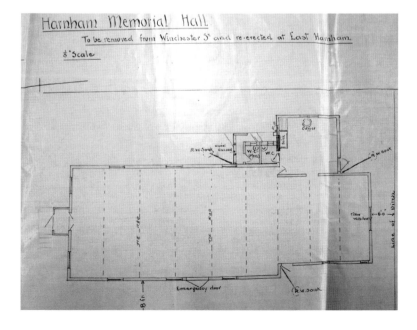

an of hall for
arnham WSA
23/760/188

be considerably lowered. Close to where the organ stood is now a more convenient entrance porch. Various appurtenances were added then, and at later dates, on the further side. However, an original pointed church window frame can still be seen from the outside, to the south of the porch, and is just visible to the right of the altar in the photograph.

Very few of the numerous 'tin tabernacles' built in Victorian times have survived to the present day. In 2010 the Harnham example was given a further lease of life with extensive refurbishment to both the main structure and the internal fittings. It is in constant use for community groups and events, and the annual Service of Remembrance in November is held there, a fitting reminder of its origin as a place of worship.

This article is based on three pieces which were first published in the *Parish of Harnham Magazine*, November & December 2010, and January 2011.

Acknowledgements

Jeremy 'Frogg' Moody (Timezone Publishing) and George Fleming, Salisbury historians, who first identified the Harnham Hall as the former Mission Church, and for details of the Eileen O'Leary connection; Jeremy Moody, for the photograph of the Mission Church interior; Harnham Women's Institute, for permission to use items from their *Scrapbook of Harnham*; Harnham Memorial Hall Management Committee for use of the 1920 *Indenture* and other information.

Bibliography

East & West Harnham Parish Magazine, Oct 1920. Purchase of the Mission Church and grand opening of the Hall. Inserted in *Scrapbook of Harnham*

SJL, 24 May 1919 p 9, report of public meeting to launch Harnham War Memorial Fund

STM, 24 September 1920, p5, an account of the opening of the Hall and its previous history as a church

WSA 776/970 *Indenture, 1920*. Purchase of land on which to build the hall

WSA G23/760/188 Building Regulations, Applications and Plans, Parish hall, rear of church, E Harnham War Memorial Comm[ittee], 1920

Ordnance Survey map of Salisbury, 1881, 66.11.25 showing Mission Church in Winchester Street

Scrapbook of Harnham, 1954-6. Harnham Women's Institute

11 Schools at East and West Harnham

Jane Howells

Before the middle of the 19th century it is unclear where, if at all, the children of East and West Harnham were educated. In the 1851 census there were 94 children in the two villages described as 'scholars' though that label does not necessarily mean they were attending a formal school. While the city of Salisbury in the early decades of the 1800s was generously provided with educational places for its children, and for those from further afield, not all the surrounding villages were so fortunate.

In 1833 the returns to an Educational Enquiry of the House of Commons stated for West Harnham 'the children of this parish attend schools in Salisbury'. Using that source it is not possible to distinguish information about East Harnham from that for Britford where there were 'two Day and Sunday Schools in which 64 children of both sexes are instructed'.[1] One of those two might well have been in East Harnham, or accessible to Harnham children.

Less than a decade later the Rev Edward Feild (sic), Inspector of National Schools, surveyed 'the state of Parochial Education in the Diocese of Salisbury'.[2] Unfortunately the returns on individual parishes sent to the Diocesan Secretary have not survived[3] but Rev Feild visited Britford on 2 June 1840 where he found 32 boys and girls attending school. In general terms he concluded 'the principles of education in the large and the true sense of the word are wisely considered and well understood ... in Your Lordship's Diocese'.[4]

Schooling for children of poorer families was available in many ways, so even if there is little evidence in directories or newspapers of formal establishments that does not mean they were receiving no tuition, at least at a basic level. Sunday Schools, 'evening schools', and 'venture' enterprises were widespread: 'throughout Britain large numbers of private day schools were provided by the working classes for the working classes',[5] and it was not unusual for these to be operated in conjunction with another business, as will be demonstrated. Education features strongly, if sometimes very briefly, in surviving working class autobiographies and diaries, and a common thread is the powerful effect of this experience. In the first half of the century working parents had the freedom to choose to send their children to school or not. Schooling was a commodity that was purchased by hard-earned family wages, it was therefore valued, but might also have to be sacrificed to other pressing needs in the household economy.[6] As will be seen below, even when enrolled in a school, a child's attendance could be erratic due to being needed for hay making, or to mind younger siblings.

William Small writing in 1881 about his childhood in Harnham in the 1820s, recalled in detail the decisions that were made about where he and his brothers and sisters should go to school. He began 'as early as I could walk' at Betsy Biddlecombe's at East Harnham. Unfortunately it has not been possible to identify Betsy Biddlecome with certainty. Elizabeth Anne Biddlecombe occupied a house in East Harnham that was certified as a meeting house in 1827, making a link with the nonconformist community there that included the Smalls.[7] She was described as a sempstress, aged 65, at the time of the 1841 census, so could also have been running a 'dame school'. James Biddlecombe had a boys' school in the Close, and was advertising in the *Salisbury Journal* 3 January 1830, and it is feasible that a female relative taught very young children at the same place. Thomas Biddlecombe was a shopkeeper in Harnham, recorded in a directory of 1830, and again a 'dame school' is a not unlikely adjunct to that.

William's brother George and their sisters Elizabeth and Henrietta all attended several schools, including one run by Ann Naish at the Rose & Crown Inn. Samuel Naish was the publican and he was succeeded by Charlotte Naish, probably his widow. One of their daughters was named Ann, so maybe the schoolmistress was Samuel's sister, taking advantage of the well-known location and spacious premises of the Rose & Crown. Interestingly, the same Ann Naish was later working as a milliner at Mrs Griffith's establishment on the New Canal where Henrietta Small learnt the trade.

By 1859 both West and East Harnham had a school, described by the Rev William Warburton in his 'Account of all Day Schools for the children of the labouring classes in the County of Wilts'. At East Harnham a new school had been opened in 1853. About 30 West Harnham children attended 'a tidy school, under a mistress of humble attainments, held in a roadside cottage'. Conditions there must have deteriorated, as looking back in 1863 Rev Chancellor Lear described it thus:

> he could testify to the wretchedness of the cottage in which the school was held. It was so open to the outer air that to inspect the school you ran the risk of catching a bad cold. But then there was an antidote; part of the school was held upstairs and part down, so that you could exercise yourself and the children by running up and down stairs when you felt cold.[8]

The occasion for his speech was the opening of a new West Harnham school to replace the cottage. This paper will now follow the fortunes of these two purpose-built Victorian schools over their first one hundred years, separately until the interwar years of the 20th century, and then together as their histories become increasingly entwined.

East Harnham School 1850s to 1950s

Mr and Mrs Edward Everett lived at The Cliff, Harnham.[9] He was a county court judge, and prominent citizen. On his death in 1870 the *Salisbury Journal's* obituary stated 'by the death of Mr Everett the poor of Harnham have lost a liberal benefactor'.[10] But it was particularly to Emma Everett that

East Harnham was indebted for the new school. Established in 1853 'the school [was] entirely managed by Mrs Everett of The Cliff East Harnham at her own private expense', having been 'built by Mr and Mrs Everett ... on Lord Folkestone's ground (by his permission)'.[11] The new school, adjoining All Saints churchyard, was constructed of Calne stone and flint, with a tile roof, and was stated ten years later to be in 'very good' condition. There was a single schoolroom[12], 36 x 20 feet, and 14 feet high, with three windows and a fireplace, plus a small side room, two 'offices' and a coal cellar. Today the building is a private house, but gives a clear impression of the original school. Mary Ann Rogers was the schoolmistress, appointed at Michaelmas 1853. She was then aged 25 and had trained as a teacher at the Salisbury Diocesan Training School, and subsequently worked for two years in Gillingham. Mrs Rogers received a salary in 1862 of £48 10s per annum and had a monitor as assistant. Attendance was on average between 45 and 50 children, boys, girls and infants.

The school received its first parliamentary grant in 1865,[13] but seems to have continued to be supported by Mrs Everett until her death in 1888. In 1893 the land and buildings were conveyed to the Salisbury Diocesan Board of Finance by Rev Charles Henry Everett 'for ever hereafter [to] be held enjoyed and used as a school for poor persons of and in the parish of East Harnham'.[14] When the Salisbury city boundary was extended to include East Harnham in 1904 the school came under the jurisdiction of the Local Education Authority, but retained its status as a Church of England school.[15]

In addition to financing the foundation and running of the school, Emma Everett arranged an 'annual feast'. The event in 1857 was reported in the *Salisbury Journal* thus: 'The day was very fine, and the children, after engaging in amusements provided for them, partook of tea, after which rewards of merit were distributed for their good conduct during the past year' and commented 'the number of children has much increased, a fact which proves that the parents are now beginning to appreciate the educational labours bestowed upon their offspring'.[16]

From the log books which began in February 1863 we discover the daily round of school life, arrivals and departures of teachers, and the comments of inspectors. There were days when 'nothing particular occurred' and others when 'some of the elder children were very troublesome, especially the boys',[17] to national events such as in 1935 when the school was closed for the Silver Jubilee.[18] Emily Adams was appointed Assistant Teacher early in 1863 and progressed in her career sufficiently so that she left in June 1870 'to take a situation of which she will be Mistress'.[19] An inspection report of 1872 stated 'the school is in fair order and has passed a fairly good general examination'. Mrs Rogers served as the mistress for nearly 20 years, as did Mary Jane More, appointed April 1874. Numbers of children remained around 60-70 for the second half of the 19th century with always a discrepancy between the total registered, and actual and average attendance. For example in December 1874 there were 76 on the books, 55 actually present and average attendance was 54; in May 1885 the figures were 73, 62 and 50 respectively.[20] These differences could be attributed to illness, the weather, and to demands on the children from family and work commitments. Diocesan inspectors were generally pleased with what they found on their regular visits. In 1874 'this school is conscientiously taught by the schoolmistress ...', 1878 'the second standard showed great intelligence in their answers', and two years later 'the children had a good understanding and knowledge, and do much credit to their teachers'.[21]

Miss Emily Grace Jerrim was appointed as mistress in charge when the school opened for the new academic year in September 1901. At first all went well, reports were good, and numbers of children were maintained. She noted some innovative lessons in what we would now call local studies: 'This afternoon St IV, V and VI were taken along the Bishop's Walk and made to study the view (1) geographically, (2) historically and (3) as an object lesson'.[22]

In 1904 Miss Jerrim was paid £93 a year, assistant teacher Miss Florence Goodfellow received £30, and early in 1905 Miss Ivy Bailey arrived as a second supplementary teacher, also on £30 per annum 'until the result of the King's Scholarship exam is known'.[23] Two months later Florence's salary was increased to £35, and Ivy's to £40, and the wages of the cleaner were raised from 1s 3d to 2s 3d per week.[24] His Majesty's Inspector (HMI) reporting for year ending March 1905 stated 'the work has improved in several particulars during the year and the progress made by the children is very satisfactory. The infants are nicely taught and are doing well'.[25]

However the children and their teachers were working in increasingly dilapidated buildings, to the extent that by the end of 1905 they were considered 'in urgent need of repair, alteration and improvement to make them reasonably fit for continued occupation as a school'.[26] Amongst the demands sent by the Education Committee to the Managers were that the roof be made watertight, floors be repaired, ceilings and walls be distempered, offices be painted and lime-whited, proper ventilation be provided, boundary walls be made safe, and entrance gates repaired. Over £800 was approved for this work.[27] Only 20 years later there was need for further repairs to the roof, floors and drains, and more re-decoration. This time the Managers applied to the National Society for a grant of £10 in addition to the funds raised locally, but the correspondent, Rev A E Dru, explained two reasons why this was causing them difficulties: as the parish adjoined the city 'the Cathedral and other city churches receive support which would come to us ordinarily' and 'some church folk in the parish will not support the church school as they think it should be handed over to LEA'.[28]

Diocesan Inspectors continued to be complimentary about what they found at East Harnham school, commenting for example in 1918 that 'this is a thoroughly satisfactory school, There is a feeling of brightness and keenness about it. The children seemed very interested in their work. They answered readily and sensibly with very little vague irrelevant guessing'. In 1921 they said that 'the general tone of this school is excellent. The children are under kindly discipline and there is a distinct mark of reverence ... The school generally gave one the impression that the religion taught was having its effect

on the lives of the children' and in 1922 that 'the children in all the groups are well informed and capable of making intelligent use of the information they possess'.[29]

However, at the same time HMI was issuing very critical reports. Miss Jerrim copied the words of the inspector G R Purdie Esq into the log book:

> The condition of this school is unsatisfactory. Though the children are orderly and behave fairly well, it is obvious that the elder children are not making sufficient effort to ensure reasonable progress in any of their lessons. This is especially the case of the boys in Class 1 whose work in Reading, Composition and Arithmetic is extremely bad ... [infants] the children are very backward but the new teacher is beginning to interest them and to secure attention and she is teaching the class on sound lines.[30]

These remarks, and much more on the same lines, stimulated a spirited defence by the Managers to the Salisbury Education Committee, largely based on sweeping social generalisations that would be extraordinary to write in more recent times:

> The school is practically a county school, the children being chiefly those of labourers, not artisans, and consequently intellectually duller.

> The more intelligent children in East Harnham, even of labourers, are now sent to Salisbury schools, chiefly St Thomas's, the duller children being retained.

Of the 90 children in the school, 35 to 40 are not East Harnham children but come from West Harnham which is an agricultural parish and under county council supervision, or from Dogdean which is a part of Britford.

It happens that at the present time the class with the worst report, the First Class of boys, is mainly composed of West Harnham children.

We regret that Arithmetic and English Composition are poor, but we maintain that under the circumstances this is unavoidable.

The Managers have the highest confidence in the headmistress and her assistants.

It must have been a relief to Miss Jerrim to read the final point, after such a disheartening report. She persisted with her efforts, and there were some 'indications of improvement' by 1926. A few years later there were more difficulties when numbers on roll fell. Discussions by the Education Committee and the Managers included the possibility of amalgamating the schools, and transferring staff elsewhere in the city, and by the early 1930s this was exacerbated by demands for strict economy of spending, and further problems with the building. In 1928 13 children of junior age were transferred from West Harnham school, which then became for infants only. Falling rolls continued to be a challenge, until in 1931 West Harnham closed and for the start of the new school year all the Harnham children attended East Harnham school.

Ten years after the Managers had felt it necessary to excuse the school's results of the grounds of having dull children from West Harnham, they were receiving 'experimental teaching' by a group of students from the Training College, children were taken to the Museum to see the 'old farm room' and four students came to East Harnham 'to see details of managing a rural school'. [31] On more positive notes such as these, Miss Jerrim completed her lengthy reign as headmistress and was replaced in April 1935 by Kathleen Ellaby.

The children were described as 'alert and industrious' by HMI in April 1937, but before long a new problem arose –

ast Harnham Junior
chool Mrs Ponting's
lass 1956 (private
ollection)

East Harnham Junior School Mrs Ponting's Class 1956 (private collection)

overcrowding – made worse from the Autumn of 1939 by the arrival of evacuees, and new constraints about numbers who could be taught together under air raid precaution rules. From 76 children in September 1937, the numbers rose to 96 in May 1939, 117 by November 1940, and 139 in May 1941. Classes were held in the parish hall, for which the LEA paid 5s per day, but the school had to work around the regular bookings by the Women's Institute and the Mothers' Union, and later they also used the Girl Guides' Hut in the Close.[32]

Following the opening in 1948 of another school at West Harnham for infants, East Harnham reverted to taking only juniors, and there began a new era of the two schools working in parallel, if not as closely as HMI might sometimes wish. Change was confirmed in 1955 when Miss Ellaby retired and Arthur Wood took over the following year, with 147 children, and 'much new equipment ordered, but there was still a deficiency of essential materials'.[33] By 1960 it was stated that 'conditions in this school have considerably improved ... the children ... work industriously and have a regard for good standards of work. They are friendly and well-mannered'.[34]

West Harnham School 1860s to 1950s

The poor condition of the 'wayside cottage' that was the only school for West Harnham children until the 1860s has already been mentioned. Its inadequacies were reiterated when appeals and applications were made to fund a replacement. The National Society was told it was 'almost in ruins'.[35] A

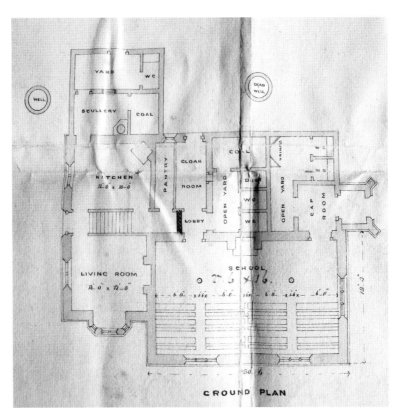

West Harnham scho
ground plan 1862.
WSA 782/53

CROUND PLAN

memorial for a government grant was addressed 'to the Lords
of the Committee of Council on Education' in February
1862, pleading special grounds of (1) the great want long
experienced by the parish of a suitable school, and (2) the
great poverty of the parish which contains no inhabitants of
wealth to help forward the work'.[36] In this document West
Harnham was described as having a population of 285, with
the labouring population employed as agricultural labourers,
plus four farmers, one miller, one butcher and one dairyman
and their families. Within 2 miles were the schools at East
Harnham and Netherhampton.[37] They anticipated an annual
income of £6.10s in school pence and £18 in subscriptions
and donations. Contributors so far included Lord Folkstone
at Longford Castle, Mr Jervoise at the Moat, Britford, Messrs
Fitzgerald, Gregory, Whickes, and Blake from West Harnham;
plus the land of the site from the Earl of Pembroke. A grant of
£120 was made.

The new school went ahead, at the junction of

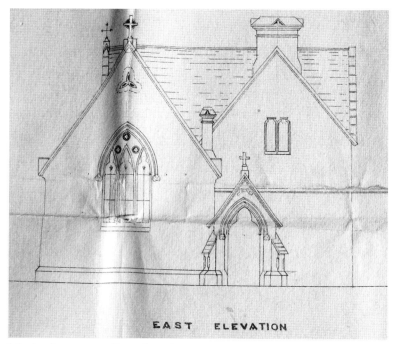

EAST ELEVATION

Netherhampton Road and Lower Street, 'a remarkably pretty building in the Decorated style, designed by S Clarke Esq, architect of Salisbury, fronted entirely in Bath stone.'[38]

In May 1863 Rev Pollard made a further application to the National Society for aid towards the 'Supply of Books, Materials and Apparatus'. This time he explained, in addition to the general poverty of the parish, that the Farmers 'are all Dissenters and contribute not a shilling to the school, or any other charitable institutions in the parish, though the landed proprietors are liberal and support the school fairly'.[39]

When Rev Chancellor Lear opened the school in September 1863, as well as thanking everyone who had contributed, he

then expressed a hope that, having such good schools, the parishioners would take heed to make good use of them. He trusted that the farmers of the parish would value that which he knew by experience farmers did value, viz., a good, sound education for their labourers. He hoped that parents would deny themselves not only to send their children but to send them regularly; that Master Johny would not be left at home for "tattie picking", and Miss Sally for baby nursing ... he then turned to the children, and reminded them that their

Salisbury races, measl
and whooping cough
West Harnham
school log book
May 23 1884, WSA
F8/500/137/1/2

duty was not only to come to school and prove themselves apt scholars, but that they must carry home what they learned ...[40]

Everyone then enjoyed 'an ample supply of tea and cake'.

Daily life at the school was established into a routine on traditional lines for the time: 'in the afternoon the boys received lessons in Writing and Arithmetic, and the girls did Needlework'.[41] The first HMI was confident that 'there is every prospect of this school doing remarkably well under the care of the present mistress who has been in charge of it but three months'.[42]

In December 1865 Mary Morris replaced Ellen Chalk and for the third quarter of the 19th century, in contrast to the experience of East Harnham, there were frequent changes of staff. This was commented on by HMI.[43] In 1867 it was said 'the discipline of the schools is v good and the mistress shows considerable ability as a teacher'.[44] However 'payments by results' was seen in action when in the following year 'the grant [was] reduced by one-tenth ... for faults in instruction in Arithmetic.[45]

Mrs Sarah Chick[46] took over on 1 January 1869, and brought in some new ideas, such as spellings being issued each night to be learned at home, but the problems of running a small rural school continued:

> One of the elder girls left to learn her mother's trade – that of a tailoress[47]
> Two children kept at home to amuse the younger ones[48]
> During the present month a girl in the First Class has left the parish to go to service, and two boys have left to mind cows[49]

[school broke up for Harvest Holidays, many children] have been employed during this week carrying their father's dinner[50]

Sarah Chick left in 1873, and returned three years later to remain until 1895, finally departing in reflective mood:

I have spent many happy years here but have long felt a younger Mistress than I now am would be preferable. Some of the children I dearly love and have been treated as their Mother more than their Teacher. I wish the greatest possible success to this school and parish. I feel very grateful to Parson and People and shall ever have kindly feelings towards all.[51]

By the early years of the new century, the mistress was in charge who would be there for the next 35 years. Alice Barber lived in the school house and had as boarders Amelia and Ellen Board who taught at East Harnham.[52] 1901 saw momentous national events reflected locally: 'As Edward VII was proclaimed King in Salisbury this morning, the children were allowed to leave at 11.25'[53] and 18 months later 'this school will be closed this afternoon because of the Coronation Procession in Salisbury'.[54]

Numbers of children at West Harnham were rising while those at East Harnham fell. HMI in 1903 commented that 'The

ject lessons,
st Harnham
ool log book
ril 26 1896, WSA
500/137/1/3

Object Lessons 1896.
Infant Department.

1.	Money	11.	Clock Face	21.	Dog
2.	Umbrella	12.	Frost	22.	Kindness to Animals
3.	Elephant	13.	Sea-Shore	23.	Ostrich
4	Camel	14.	Coal	24.	Donkey
5	Cotton	15.	An Egg	25.	Cleanliness
6	Silkworm	16.	Day & Night	26.	Snail
7	Cork	17.	Goat	27.	Cow
8	Tea	18.	An Apple	28.	A Tree
9	Squirrel	19.	Horse	29.	Coverings of Animals
10	Milk	20.	Seasons.	30.	Water.

numbers have increased and for the teaching to be effective a classroom is now required. Good order is maintained and the teachers have worked hard, but satisfactory progress cannot be made under the present conditions.[55]

When the school opened in the autumn of 1904, 15 children in the upper standards (IV, V and VI) had been transferred to East Harnham, so Salisbury Education Committee acquired the two schools concentrating on different levels, a distinction that would be reflected throughout much of the 20th century. In 1906 Wiltshire County Council asked for a description of the school, and Rev Hill replied sending a plan with measurements and a photograph, showing accommodation for 50 children. They progressed into the 1920s, despite difficulties such as measles and chicken pox, and in the late summer of 1916 scarlet fever and diphtheria resulting in the death of one child. In 1919 there was noted progress since 1914, and by 1926 a considerable difference in tone – the HMI very positive: 'The orderliness of the school and the interest of the children in their work continue to be commendable features ... Moreover there has been a gradual and real advance in the results of the instruction ...'.[56]

Further change was to come shortly when in 1928 West Harnham formally became a school for infants only, but discussion about its future continued, as the number of pupils on roll continued to decline. Despite an encouraging diocesan report that 'the work is carefully and conscientiously done, and

West Harnham Infant School 1965, in Nissen huts. Harnham Women's Institute Scrapbook 1965

the children are all bright and responsive' the school closed in September 1931.[57] The building was let, and caused some concern to the National Society, that the Earl of Pembroke (having given the land for the school in the first place) might claim a reversion of the property; that the proceeds of the rent were being applied to East Harnham school (strictly speaking not permitted); and the schoolroom should be being used for some alternative educational purpose, such as a library or reading room, evening classes, religious instruction, or physical instruction by means of a gymnasium.[58] The whole building was sold in 1951.[59]

During the second world war and immediately afterwards, as mentioned above, pressure of numbers on the premises at East Harnham increased. In 1948 a 'new' West Harnham County Infants' School for 120 children was opened in Suffolk Road, housed in two adapted ex-military Nissen huts, later joined by a new classroom. The lavatory block was across the road, 'peculiarly disturbing in an Infants school, since the young children cannot be infallibly regular in their habits'.[60] Initially surrounded by a building site erecting an estate of pre-fabricated housing, the school quickly filled with children from the area.

Conclusion from the 1950s

Throughout the 1950s both Harnham Schools were operating in far from ideal surroundings, and the Local Education Authority received comments and recommendations from HMI to this effect for many years. The 1953 HMI report on East Harnham concluded 'few palliatives for the discouraging physical conditions are possible until such time as a new school can be built. It remains therefore for the Headmistress and her staff to respond to the challenge of heavy difficulty with courage and wisdom'.[61] Though, as mentioned above, there were some subsequent improvements. At West Harnham five years later, HMI hoped 'that the new school can be provided before the old Army huts wear out completely', but despite that 'it is to the credit of the school that many [of the children] become cheerful, friendly, and responsible people with considerable interest in the work they do'. [62]

Immediately post-war there were heavy demands on local authority finances, not least from other schools in equally difficult surroundings, plus housing, roads, utilities and more. From 1950 resolutions were passed regularly that new schools at Harnham be included in the Building Programme, to no avail. Land below the Hill, accessed from the top of Saxon Road, had been earmarked at an early date. It was purchased in 1952 then let on short term leases to farmers for the next decade, always with the condition that if building could start the site would be required at short notice.[63]

Eventually the infants moved into a new building of innovative design ('whimsical' was how it was described by HMI in 1974) in 1965 and the Juniors' new school followed three years later. Mr Wood retired at Christmas 1969, and Miss King retired in 1976 after 24 years as headmistress of the infants. Since then the two schools, while maintaining their separate names and identities, have worked increasingly closely together to become the successful establishments they are today.[64]

Bibliography

Langmead & Evans, 1897, *Directory of Salisbury & District 1897-8,* Langmead & Evans

Stephens, W B, 1999, *Education in Britain 1750-1914,* Palgrave Macmillan

Education Enquiry. Abstracts of Answers and Returns, House of Commons 24 May 1833 England & Wales. Vol III

VCH *Wilts* 6

Vincent, D, 1981, *Bread, Knowledge and Freedom: a study in Nineteenth Century Working Class Autobiography,* Methuen

At the National Archives

TNA ED7/132 Preliminary Statement East Harnham Church of England mixed school 19 Dec 1862

TNA ED103/95 school number 503

TNA ED21/42456 HMI reports

At the Church of England Record Centre

NS/3/1/12 National Society Annual Reports 1839-40

NS/7/1/5850 East Harnham school file 1893-1975

NS/7/1/5851 West Harnham school file 1890-1971

In WSA at the WSHC

WSA D/625/1, 1840 surviving returns to diocese-wide survey

WSA F2/600/179/2 Properties and sites correspondence, Salisbury Harnham CE Junior School, 1947-54 copy of indenture

WSA F8/230/2/4 Cuttings book of minutes relating to school premises, 1940-62.

WSA F8/300/147 Harnham CE School HMI report 1953

WSA F8/300/148 Harnham County Infants HMI reports 1949-93

WSA F8/300/149 Harnham County Juniors HMI reports 1953-93

WSA F8/500/136/1/1 E Harnham CE School log book 1863-73

WSA F8/500/136/1/2 E Harnham CE School log book 1898-1931

WSA F8/500/136/1/3 E Harnham CE School log book 1931-74

WSA F8/500/137/1/1 W Harnham CE School log book 1863-82

WSA F8/500/137/1/2 W Harnham CE School log book 1882-92

WSA F8/500/137/1/3 W Harnham CE School log book 1892-1906

WSA F8/500/137/1/4 W Harnham CE School log book 1906-31

WSA F8/600/136/1/3/1 Harnham Junior CE School Managers Minutes 1904-85

WSA F8/600/136/1/12/1 Harnham Junior CE School Diocesan Inspection Report Book 1874-1935

WSA F8/870/1 Salisbury Education Committee Minute Book 1903-05

Notes

1   Education Enquiry, 1038, 1030

2   The instructions he received are reminiscent of the advice given at the time of modern OFSTED inspections: '…you will be careful to explain that the purpose of your visit is only to assist them in the completion of their own design, not so much to expose errors as to promote improvements, to control as to persuade, to censure as to encourage, in short to shew how the well-being, moral and religious, physical and intellectual, of the rising generation, may be most effectually promoted'. p27

3   Except for Whiteparish and Sutton Waldron. WSA D/625/1 1840

4   NS/3/1/12 National Society Annual Reports 1839-40 p146

5   Stephens, 1

6   Vincent 1981, p96, 101, 103

7   See chapter 7, Newman

8   *SJL* 26 Sept 1863 p7

9   See picture p109

10   *SJL* 29 Jan 1870 p8

11   TNA ED7/132 Preliminary Statement East Harnham Church of England mixed school 19 Dec 1862, and information in the rest of this paragraph

12   Later divided into two by a sliding wood and glass screen WSA F8/500/136/1/3, 11 September 1934

13   VCH *Wilts* 6 p167

14   WSA F2/600/179/2 copy of indenture

15   Under the 1902 Education Act Salisbury City was the LEA responsible for elementary schools. See chapter 9 for the boundary extension.

16   *SJL* 3 October 1857 p5

17   WSA F8/500/136/1/1 26 Feb 1863 and 16 Feb 1863

18   WSA F8/500/136/1/3, 6 May 1935

19   WSA F8/500/136/1/1 9 Feb 1863 and 17 June 1870

20   WSA F8/600/136/1/12/1

21   *Ibid*

22   WSA F8/500/136/1/2, 24 September 1901

23   WSA F8/870/1 Salisbury Education Committee Minute Book p271, 291

24   *Ibid* p318, 332

25   *Ibid* p360

26   *Ibid* p442

27   *Ibid* p443

28   NS/7/1/5850

29   WSA F8/600/136/1/12/1 Diocesan Report Book 1874-1935. TNA ED21/42456

30   WSA F8/500/136/1/2, 27 April 1922. This followed a similarly worded HMI report in 1919 TNA ED21/42456 when arithmetic in Class I was considered 'a total failure', though 'the children are in good order and the relationship between them and their teachers is pleasant and friendly'.

31   WSA F8/500/136/1/3, Feb – March 1932

32   WSA F8/600/136/1/3/1

33   WSA F8/500/136/1/3, 9 January 1956

34   WSA F8/300/149

35   NS/7/1/5851

36   TNA ED103/95 school number 503

37   I have found no evidence of West Harnham children attending Netherhampton school though those from the west of the parish may well have done so.

38   *SJL* 26 September 1863 p7

39   NS/7/1/5851

40   *SJL* 26 September 1863 p7

41   WSA F8/500/137/1/1 12 January 1866

42   *Ibid* 19 November 1863

43   *Ibid* 21 December 1875

44   *Ibid* 5 December 1867

45   *Ibid* 17 November 1868

46   Sarah Chick came from Weymouth, and was married to a cabinet maker from Taunton. They had a daughter and three sons (1881

census). As Sarah Talbot she had trained at Salisbury and qualified in 1861. When she referred to her age on departure, she would have been in her mid-fifties.

47   WSA F8/500/137/1/1, 21 January 1868
48   *Ibid* 15 April 1869
49   *Ibid* March 1875
50   WSA F8/500/137/1/2
51   WSA F8/500/137/1/3, 18 November 1895
52   1901 census, Langmead & Evans *Directory* p220-1
53   WSA F8/500/137/1/3, 28 January 1901
54   *Ibid* 18 July 1902
55   *Ibid* October 1903
56   WSA F8/500/137/1/4
57   *Ibid*
58   NS/7/1/5851 correspondence 1937-8
59   VCH *Wilts* 6, p168
60   WSA F8/300/148
61   WSA F8/300/147, 16 November 1953
62   WSA F8/300/148, 17 February 1958
63   WSA F8/230/2/4 Cuttings Book and F2/600/179/2
64   Recent OFSTED reports classify both as 'good' schools; comments on social media sites such as Facebook indicate fond memories from past pupils.

Michael Cowan (right) explaining the finer points of the watermeadows to a group of BALH members on a guided visit to Salisbury, 2007

12 Michael Cowan: Administrator and General Secretary, British Association for Local History

(a profile published on the occasion of his retirement
The Local Historian *Vol 33 No 3 August 2003 p 130)*

David Dymond

'Chairman, I think we had better move on'. At many meetings which I chaired in the years 1996-2001, those words wafted softly but authoritatively into my left ear. They came from our General Secretary, Michael Cowan, who was always conscious of the length of an agenda and of the time allowed for it. I'm sure it is true to say that for the last fourteen years or so Mike has been so identified with BALH, so central a figure in our affairs, that we all find it difficult to believe that he has been forced into sudden retirement. The reason, as most members of the Association will have heard by now, is that in 2002 he was diagnosed with brain cancer, and finally had to give up his duties on 7 March 2003. In recent months he has undergone major treatment in hospital, but he remains characteristically philosophical and cheerful, positively enjoying some aspects of his new-found leisure (such as opera, preferably Wagner, played very loud).

Mike was born in 1935 and brought up in Surrey. He went to

Kingston Grammar School (of which he wrote a short history), and then proceeded to the Royal Military Academy at Sandhurst and Staff College at Camberley. He served in the Royal Army Service Corps (now Royal Logistic Corps) for thirty-two years, and during that time was posted to far-flung places such as Libya, Trucial Oman, Singapore and North Borneo. From 1976 he was based in the UK, and that gave him the opportunity to use the War Office Library, to revive his interest in English history and to gain an OU degree. He finally retired from the Ministry of Defence in 1986 with the rank of lieutenant-colonel, but with characteristic energy soon built up a new pattern of voluntary and paid work. For example, he became secretary of the Wiltshire Archaeological Society and part-time director of the Wiltshire Life Society and their museum at Avebury; he also did management work for organisations such as Mencap and Relate. Over the years several publications appeared under his name, including articles on military memorials in Salisbury Cathedral and on Wiltshire water-meadows. He also edited a volume of letters written by a nineteenth-century architect, which was published by the Wiltshire Record Society.

Mike's involvement with BALH began in 1987 when he was elected to Council. In 1989 he was elected honorary secretary, in succession to David Short. At that time the Association had just moved from Cromford in Derbyshire to a new home offered by the publishers Phillimore at Chichester. As a way of building up the strength of the organisation, Mike was appointed our part-time paid administrator in 1990. Five years later BALH was confident enough to strike out on its own again, with its official address at Mike's home near Salisbury. Since then, on a part-time basis, he has skilfully run the day-to-day affairs of the Association (made all the more onerous in recent years because of the lack of an honorary treasurer), kept the publishing programme on course, arranged a variety of events, serviced our regular meetings, given advice and information to officers and Council, and carried the banner of the Association wherever he went. His job was renamed 'general secretary' in 1998.

In my time as chairman, I found Mike's support utterly invaluable. Yes, some people may be put off by military smartness (I don't think I have ever seen Mike without a tie), a somewhat brisk manner and a reluctance to talk about himself, but how else is someone in his position to steer a crowd of woolly-headed historians? His basic attitude was always: tell me what you want to achieve in terms of objectives and policies, and I will deliver. He has little patience with committees who spend their time 'counting the paper clips' (his own phrase). Yet anyone who works with Mike soon comes to appreciate his dry humour, usually delivered with a chuckle. And in case you think that Mike is always laconic, let me also tell you that he is capable of extending a telephone call to its ultimate limits. In my time as chairman, I had to eat many a cold supper because my briefing for a forthcoming meeting went on for well over an hour. It was no good my saying 'I know about that', because I had to be taken through the entire agenda, in considerable detail. If necessary, in the light of our conversation, arrangements could be 'tweaked' (one of Mike's favourite words).

To supplement my own impressions, I have talked to several other people who have worked with Mike in the last decade or more. They are all agreed that his contribution has been vital. 'Without Mike, BALH would have foundered', said one. Two others homed in on his methods: 'an organisational genius' who 'brought real efficiency to BALH ... a kind of military Jeeves'. 'He is reluctant to explain how he was to deliver his black arts, but deliver he always did'. Mike himself tells me that the three aspects of the job he is most proud of are the establishment of the annual Phillimore Lecture, the setting up of the Local History Awards (for publication and for service) and the completion of the Index Project which has unlocked so much valuable material in *The Local Historian*.

We are deeply grateful to Mike for years of hard work, enthusiasm and dedication to the cause of local history. Members, I'm sure, will want to join me in sending good wishes to him, his wife Jennifer and their son and two daughters. A good piece of news announced at the last meeting of Council is that Mike has accepted an invitation to become a member of the Development Committee. With that link, we can continue to enjoy the benefit of his expertise and experience.

'Horticulture and agriculture in Harnham'

PINK FEAST.

THE ANNUAL FEAST will be held at the Rose and Crown Inn, East Harnham, on Wednesday the 23d inst. with the following PRIZES :—

Any person producing the twelve best Flowers, having been in his own possession three months, a Piece of Plate, value - - - - - £.1 10 0

For the twelve second best Flowers, ditto - - 0 18 0
For the twelve third best Flowers, ditto - - 0 10 6
For the six best Seedlings - - - - 0 7 6

N. B. Dinner on table at two o'clock.

614]

THOMAS ROLES,
WILLIAM HEALE, } Stewards.
JAMES TAYLER,

East Harnham, Salisbury, June 2, 1802.

Pink Feast is from *Salisbury Journal* 7 June 1802

EAST HARNHAM.

HOP PICKING.—The annual hop picking at Mr. Samuel Naish's Avon Brewery Hop Ground, took place on Thursday last. A spacious marquee, decorated with flags, &c., had been erected, and the Misses Naish and a few friends entertained about 90 of the boys and girls, with their attendants, from the Alderbury Union, with a goodly supply of tea, cake, lemonade, &c. Some portion of the hop poles were placed in the tents, and were decked as a Christmas tree, with various articles as presents for the children, kindly given by Mr. T. Barnard. The Rev. C. A. Houghton was present, and looked after the wants of his little flock, who all appeared thoroughly to enjoy themselves. At the rev. gentleman's request, the children gave hearty cheers for Mr. and Mrs. S.Naish, the Misses Naish, Mr. Brownjohn, Miss Clough, Mr. George Marlow, and all the party concerned. After singing the "National Anthem," and "God bless the Prince of Wales," the party returned home, feeling themselves well rewarded for their labours.

WEST HARNHAM.

HARVEST THANKSGIVING.—A service of thanksgiving for the securing of the late harvest was held in the parish church on the evening of Thursday last, when the venerable edifice presented quite a gay appearance, being tastefully decorated with flowers, corn, fruit, &c. A large congregation assembled, and hymns of a suitable character were sung, and an impressive sermon was preached by the Rev. H. S. Pollard, M.A., from Mark iv. 28, "The full corn in the ear." Among those who took part in the service were the Revds. C. A. Houghton, E. T. Houghton, and R. Jackson. At the close of the service a collection was made on behalf of the Salisbury Infirmary.

Harvest Thanksgiving and Hop Picking are both from *Salisbury Journal* 8 September 1872

13 Michael Cowan's publications

Books

Military Memorials in Salisbury Cathedral. M Cowan,1981, revised
   1985

Floated Water Meadows in the Salisbury Area, South Wiltshire
   Industrial Archaeology Society Historical Monograph 9,
   1982

*The Letters of John Peniston, Salisbury Architect, Catholic and
   Yeomanry Officer 1823-1830*. Edited by Michael Cowan,
   WRS, 1994

*Wiltshire Water Meadows. Understanding and conserving the remains
   of a farming and engineering revolution*. Hobnob Press, 2005

*Harnham Mill, Salisbury. The oldest surviving paper mill in the
   country*. Sarum Studies 2. Hobnob Press, 2008

The Harnham Water Meadows. Sarum Studies 3. Hadrian Cook,
   Michael Cowan, Tim Tatton-Brown. Hobnob Press, 2008

Published articles

The Negotiation of Host Nations Support Agreements and the
   possible effect of organizations on their credibility, a Report
   to North Atlantic Treaty Organisation. Research carried out
   with the assistance of a NATO research fellowship grant,
   May 1981-Dec 1982

A local battle in A.D.552, *Hatcher Review*, No 11, Spring 1981

Mysterious Meadows: some aspects of the floated
   watermeadows at Great Wishford, Wiltshire, *Hatcher Review*,
   No 14, Autumn 1982

Men of the Regiment, *Wiltshire Folklife* 13, Winter 1985

The Penistons: a Salisbury Family of Catholic Architects and
   Yeomen 1770-1911. *WANHM*, Vol 80, 1986

Military Memorials in the Cathedral, *Spire* [newsletter of the
   Friends of Salisbury Cathedral], 1987

Mid-19th century "Ideal Homes" in Salisbury? *Wiltshire Folklife* 15, 1987

The Wardour Castles and their landscape, *Hatcher Review* 25, 1988

The Penistons of Salisbury: men of influence, *Wiltshire Folklife* 19, Autumn 1989

Wiltshire Ice Houses, *Wiltshire Folklife 22*, Spring 1991

What do you understand by 'Bellhanging'? *WLHF Newsletter* 27, January 1994

South West Regional Archive Council, *WLHF Newsletter* 46, May 2000

Musings on Light Pollution, *South Wiltshire Group Newsletter, CPRE,* November 2003

Are Regimental Colours Records? *WRS Newsletter*, February 2004

Are Regimental Colours Records? *The Kingsman Regimental Journal*, 2003

High Street Sheep, *Salisbury Civic Society Newsletter*, August 2004

Musings on Light Pollution. *The Newsletter, Campaign to Protect Rural England, Issue 2,* October 2004

Salisbury as a Seaport: some further debate. *Sarum Chronicle,* Issue Four, 2004

Times change. *Local History News* 80, Summer 2006

Times change. *WLHF Newsletter* 66, January 2007

Salisbury: the seaport that never was. *Sarum Chronicle*, Issue Eight, 2008

The City Ditch, Bugmore and the Bourne: an irrigation agreement and urban effluent on the periphery of Salisbury by Hadrian Cook and Michael Cowan. *WANHM,* Vol 102, 2009

Contributions

Notes, News, Issues. *Local History News*. British Association for Local History. Regular column until May 2009.

Mentioned in the foreword of *The History of Kingston Grammar School 1299-1999* by David Ward and Gordon Evans, printed in 2000. As a sixth former Michael wrote well researched articles for the *Kingstonian* magazine, referred to this history of the school.

Reviews

N D G James. Plain Soldiering: A History of the Armed Forces on Salisbury Plain. *WANHM,* Vol 82, 1988

How Devizes won the war, edited by Lorna Haycock. *WLHF Newsletter* 31, May 1995

Architects and Building Craftsmen with Work in Wiltshire, Pamela Slocombe. *WLHF Newsletter* 35, September 1996

The Old Lady on the Hill – the story of Christ Church Parish Church of Swindon, and its community 1851-2001, Brian Bridgeman and Teresa Squires. *WLHF Newsletter* 51, January 2002

Scenes from a Hampshire Childhood, Gerald Ponting. *WLHF Newsletter* 60, January 2005

Clarendon: landscape of kings, Tom Beaumont James and Christopher Gerrard. *WLHF Newsletter* 69, January 2008

Earls of Paradise: England and the dream of perfection, Adam Nicholson. *WLHF Newsletter* 71, September 2008

Newsletters/Pamphlets

Creation Festival May 1990 – an environmental Festival to promote local and worldwide conservation

The Friends of Salisbury Festival

Wiltshire Archaeological and Natural History Society

Wiltshire Wildlife

Friends of Harnham Water Meadows Trust

CPRE South Wiltshire Group Newsletter

Salisbury Civic Society

Web

www.salisburywatermeadow.fsnet.co.uk : initiation and liaison; *Michael was an enthusiastic advocate of developing electronic communication between organisations and their members*

Research Notes for Talks

The Wardour Castles and their landscape – talk given to Salisbury Local History Group, May 1985

Some aspects of the Victorian Army in Wiltshire – lecture given to the WLHF Conference, September 1985

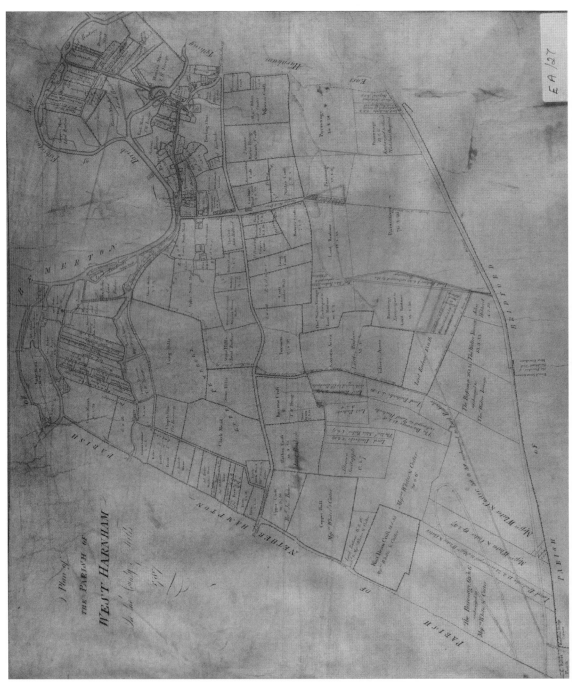

Inclosure map 1787. WSA A1/210/115/EA 27

15 Harnham in some volumes published by the Wiltshire Record Society

Jane Howells

The Wiltshire Record Society was founded, for the second time, in 1937 so in 2012 celebrated 75 years of publishing transcripts of historical documents relating to the county. Beginning as the Records Branch of the Wiltshire Archaeological & Natural History Society, in 1967 it became the Wiltshire Record Society, an independent organisation in its own right. In an earlier incarnation, a body with the same name was established in 1887,[1] under the presidency of Bishop John Wordsworth. 'A new antiquarian zeal' stirred editorial activity in the last decade or so of the19th century, particularly in the south of Wiltshire.[2] *Churchwardens Accounts of St Edmund and St Thomas Sarum 1443-1702,* edited by H J F Swayne, was published in 1896 under the Society's imprint, and the Bishop in his preface confirms 'these accounts will form the first volume of the Society's publications'.[3] Two further volumes followed: *Canonization of St Osmond* edited by A R Malden (1901) and *Cartulary of St Nicholas Hospital* edited by Christopher Wordsworth (1902). At the same time *Wiltshire Notes and Queries,* which ran from 1893 to 1916, was including indexes and some translated extracts, and there were some similar publications by individuals. WANHS itself also started work along these lines, initially within the *Magazine,* then in association with other bodies such as the British Record Society. Following a successful appeal for funds, the Society published two volumes of

The Tropenell Cartulary in 1908.[4] The First World War intervened, then renewed enthusiasm eventually resulted in the Record Society as it is today.

The modern society has produced 65 volumes over its three-quarters of a century, the numbering continuing over the change in 1967. John Chandler and Steven Hobbs have, in their papers for this volume, demonstrated the value of the cartularies mentioned above. A further small selection is introduced here, giving a few examples of information relating to Harnham with the objective of drawing attention to the rich material to be found therein. They are given in numerical order of publication. Note also the volume edited by Michael Cowan (see Introduction p 8) and Volume 64 (see Chapter 7 on William Small at Harnham).

Vol 15 1960 *Tradesmen in Early-Stuart Wiltshire* ed N J Williams

Tradesmen and women appeared in the documents transcribed in this volume because they were involved in part of the extensive administrative structure surrounding local economic activity at the time. For example fines were imposed on those who fell foul of regulations, thus in 1607 'Thomas Greene of West Harnham, victualler, and John Hill of Bemerton, for not appearing with their bread of all kinds for weighing with the standards' were fined 3s 4d each.[5] King James I was a staunch upholder of Lenten fasting. In late 1619 a proclamation was issued that Justices of the Peace should take recognisances of all inn-keepers, victuallers and the like, that they would not permit the consumption of meat on their premises during Lent the following year. It was necessary to provide two people to stand surety, and the penalties were potentially severe. So on 28 February 1620 Anthony Wilshire of Harneham, innholder gave his recognisance, with John Galley and Thomas Wilshire both glovers of Salisbury as sureties; and on the same day Ralph Justrell of Estharneham, tippler, had Giles Morgan, baker, and Rowland Warren, brewer, both of Salisbury as his.[6]

Vol 25 1971 *Abstracts of Wiltshire Inclosure Awards and Agreements* ed R E Sandell

Inclosure awards provide a snapshot of land ownership during the process of changing from collective landholding to its division into separate parcels. These abstracts are given in standard form, and provide a consistent skeleton of the information in the full awards and accompanying maps (which are noted but not reproduced in this volume). West Harnham inclosure award was dated 1787, and affected the parish of 1,179 acres. East Harnham was included with Britford.[7]

Vol 40 1985 *Wiltshire Dissenters' Meeting House Certificates and Registrations 1689 -1852* ed John Chandler

The Toleration Act of 1689, and its subsequent alterations, allowed dissenting denominations to become an accepted part of English religious life. Meeting houses were required to be registered, and this process therefore provided a record of their location, the premises used, the key people involved, and normally the denomination concerned. The earliest in Harnham was 'the dwellinghouse of John Baker in East Harnham ... Quaker ...' registered June 1703. One hundred and twenty years later the Independent or Tent Methodists were meeting in East Harnham in 'An orchard in the occupation of Samual Naish, containing one acre'. At West Harnham in 1846 'a house and premises now in the holding and occupation of Frederick Hopkins' was used by the Primitive Methodists. This volume provided valuable background information for the editors of Vol 64.[8]

Vol 52 1996 *Printed Maps of Wiltshire 1787 – 1844* ed John Chandler

The generous handful of maps reprinted in this collection

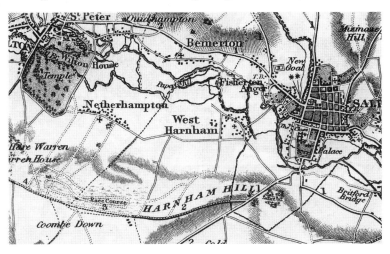

Christopher Greenwood. *Map of the County of Wilts* 1820. WRS Vol 52 p 134

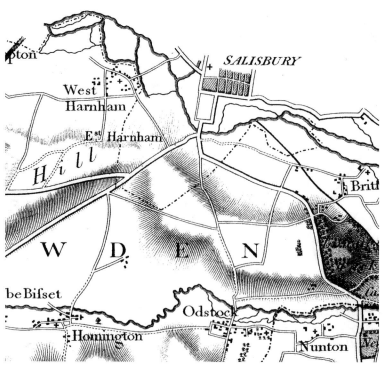

Philip Crocker. *Map of Hundreds for the History of Modern Wiltshire.* WRS Vol 52 p 173

would otherwise be difficult for the local historian to use. This accessibility more than offsets the inconvenience of their division into sometimes ridiculously small sections to fit the pages of a book. Both Christopher Greenwood in 1820 and Philip Crocker (drawn c 1821–4) show the rural nature of Harnham at that time, though Crocker completely fails to record any buildings at East Harnham.

Vol 53 1997 *Monumental Inscriptions of Wiltshire 1822* ed Peter Sherlock

Sir Thomas Phillipps organised and published this collection of epitaphs in Wiltshire churches in 1822. While incomplete and at times inaccurate it does preserve a record of many epitaphs that were subsequently destroyed. The WRS volume is, unusually, a facsimile of the original; and the language and sentiments of commemoration are a valuable characteristic for historians. At West Harnham, for example, there was an inscription 'To the Memory of Maria and Ann Kirkman, whose short Lives exhibited the true loveliness of the Female Character under the influence of Virtue and Religion. Maria died Dec. 4th 1791, Aged 22 years. Ann Died June 28th 1799, Aged 28 years.'[9]

Vol 54 1998 *The First General Entry Book of the City of Salisbury 1387-1452* **ed David R Carr**

Mike Cowan used this volume when he was tracing medieval occupants of Harnham Mill.[10] In 1424 the city authorities agreed 'William Lord to ride to London to deal with the matter of William Fyns with wise counsel for the lands and tenements of the mill in West Harnham and New Salisbury' and in 1425 'William Lord to deal with ... David Cervyngton for his estate which he claims in the lands and tenements in West Harnham later John Pynnock's'.[11]

Vol 56 2000 *Wiltshire Glebe Terriers 1588 – 1827* **ed Steven Hobbs**

It is important to realise that East Harnham was once part of the parish of Britford, so is included there in volumes such as this. The terrier (a description of the property of a benefice, setting out the sources of income for parish clergy, effectively a clergyman's title deeds) of 1615 tells us that the 'tithe hay of E Harnham common mead belongs to the parson', as does 'all tithe of all the hams lying below Harnham bridge between the river and the Cow lane'.[12]

Vol 58 2006 *Early Motor Vehicle Registration in Wiltshire 1903–1914* **ed Ian Hicks**

Residents of Harnham were amongst the citizens who took to the new form of road transport available in the early years of the 20th century. In October 1908 Ernest Blake at Oakfields Lodge, East Harnham, registered a 12 hp two cylinder 'Metallurgique' in olive green picked out in black and red.[13] The Macklin family of 'Watersmeet' were keen early motorists, James had a Scout touring car 'painted blue with white imitation cane work', and Bernard a Triumph motor cycle.[14] Alfred Fowler at The Swan Hotel ran a baby Peugeot, and across the road at East Harnham Post Office there was a yellow Mercedes lorry registered by Frederick Hand in 1920.

Vol 60 2007 *The Hungerford Cartulary* **ed J L Kirby**

The Hungerfords were a prominent Wiltshire family of the later 14th century. This is the second volume published by WRS of cartularies recording their titles to their estates. Although originally centred on Heytesbury and Farleigh Hungerford, the family's land extended far through the county. Just one example of the information available here is 'Deed of Walter de Calne, as William de Sancto Omero, knight, gave him and Isabel his wife a pasture called 'Langeham' lying lengthwise along the bank of the Avon in East Harnham between the lands and tenements of East Harnham to the south and the river bank to the north, as enclosed by ditches …'[15]

Notes
1   Thomas 2003 pxxi
2   Pugh 1953 p35
3   Swayne 1896 piii
4   Pugh 1953 p36
5   Vol 15, p7
6   Vol 15 ,p1
7   Vol 25, p80 and 32
8   Vol 40, p12, 100, 162. See also ch 7 on William Small and the Methodists of Harnham
9   Vol 53 ,p34
10   Cowan 2008 p10
11   Vol 54, p20, 122
12   Vol 56, p57
13   Vol58 ,p155
14   Vol 58, p245 and 308
15   Vol 60, p31

Index

Harnham

Harnham